Censorship & Free Speech

Editor: Danielle Lobban

Volume 418

First published by Independence Educational Publishers

The Studio, High Green

Great Shelford

Cambridge CB22 5EG

England

© Independence 2023

Copyright

This book is sold subject to the condition that it shall not,
by way of trade or otherwise, be lent, resold, hired out or otherwise
circulated in any form of binding or cover other than that in which it
is published without the publisher's prior consent.

Photocopy licence

The material in this book is protected by copyright. However, the
purchaser is free to make multiple copies of particular articles for instructional
purposes for immediate use within the purchasing institution.
Making copies of the entire book is not permitted.

ISBN-13: 978 1 86168 878 1

Printed in Great Britain

Zenith Print Group

Acknowledgements

The publisher is grateful for permission to reproduce the material in this book. While every care has been taken to trace and acknowledge copyright, the publisher tenders its apology for any accidental infringement or where copyright has proved untraceable. The publisher would be pleased to come to a suitable arrangement in any such case with the rightful owner.

The material reproduced in **issues** books is provided as an educational resource only. The views, opinions and information contained within reprinted material in **issues** books do not necessarily represent those of Independence Educational Publishers and its employees.

Images

Cover image courtesy of iStock. All other images courtesy of Freepik, Pixabay and Unsplash, except pages 8.

Additional acknowledgements

With thanks to the Independence team: Shelley Baldry, Tracy Biram, Klaudia Sommer and Jackie Staines.

Danielle Lobban

Cambridge, January 2023

Contents

Chapter 1: Censorship in the UK

Censorship in the United Kingdom: is it a problem?	1
The UK risks becoming a world leader in online censorship	4
UK government ties itself in knots over social media censorship	5
New UK 'bill of rights' exempts government from free speech protections	6
How 17th-century Britain's 'cancel culture' can help us understand the importance of free speech	8
Cancel culture: what views are Britons afraid to express?	10
Free speech 'stifled' as universities cancel record number of speakers	13
Most students think UK universities protect free speech, survey finds	14
Financial censorship	15
PayPal reinstates Free Speech Union accounts after being accused of 'politically motivated' ban	17

Chapter 2: Press Freedom

What is free press and how does it work? What is its role in a democracy?	18
European Parliament appears to censor report on press censorship in EU	20
We're fine as we are, press tells EU as Brussels plans media freedom law	21
The fine line between fake news and freedom of speech	22
How Iran is suppressing protest at the World Cup by censoring players and banning journalists.	24
Nobel Prize underscores risks to journalists and democracy	28
2021: a grim year for journalists and free speech in an increasingly turbulent and authoritarian world	29
Five questions for every newsroom to ask themselves on World Press Freedom Day	30

Chapter 3: Freedom of Expression

Freedom of expression is key to countering disinformation	32
Article 10: Freedom of expression	33
Freedom of speech? Not these days, if you're an artist in Britain	34
Salman Rushdie's battle for free speech has been lost, friends say	35
Without blasphemy the West would have no free speech	36
'It's a culture war that's totally out of control': the authors whose books are being banned in US schools	38
Whistleblowing and freedom of expression: personal rights and public wrongs	41
Further Reading/Useful Websites	42
Glossary	43
Index	44

Introduction

Censorship & Free Speech is Volume 418 in the issues series. The aim of the series is to offer current, diverse information about important issues in our world, from a UK perspective.

About Censorship & Free Speech

Freedom of expression is a universal human right and the cornerstone of a free society. All media we consume are subject to levels of censorship we are not always aware of. From banning books, to cancelling speakers at universities to detaining journalists, this book looks at different types of censorship and threats to freedom of speech in the UK and around the world.

Our sources

Titles in the issues series are designed to function as educational resource books, providing a balanced overview of a specific subject.

The information in our books is comprised of facts, articles and opinions from many different sources, including:

- Newspaper reports and opinion pieces
- Website factsheets
- Magazine and journal articles
- Statistics and surveys
- Government reports
- Literature from special interest groups.

A note on critical evaluation

Because the information reprinted here is from a number of different sources, readers should bear in mind the origin of the text and whether the source is likely to have a particular bias when presenting information (or when conducting their research). It is hoped that, as you read about the many aspects of the issues explored in this book, you will critically evaluate the information presented.

It is important that you decide whether you are being presented with facts or opinions. Does the writer give a biased or unbiased report? If an opinion is being expressed, do you agree with the writer? Is there potential bias to the 'facts' or statistics behind an article?

Activities

Throughout this book, you will find a selection of assignments and activities designed to help you engage with the articles you have been reading and to explore your own opinions. Some tasks will take longer than others and there is a mixture of design, writing and research-based activities that you can complete alone or in a group.

Further research

At the end of each article we have listed its source and a website that you can visit if you would like to conduct your own research. Please remember to critically evaluate any sources that you consult and consider whether the information you are viewing is accurate and unbiased.

Issues Online

The **issues** series of books is complimented by our online resource, issuesonline.co.uk

On the Issues Online website you will find a wealth of information, covering over 70 topics, to support the PSHE and RSE curriculum.

Why Issues Online?

Researching a topic? Issues Online is the best place to start for...

Librarians

Issues Online is an essential tool for librarians: feel confident you are signposting safe, reliable, user-friendly online resources to students and teaching staff alike. We provide multi-user concurrent access, so no waiting around for another student to finish with a resource. Issues Online also provides FREE downloadable posters for your shelf/wall/table displays.

Teachers

Issues Online is an ideal resource for lesson planning, inspiring lively debate in class and setting lessons and homework tasks.

Our accessible, engaging content helps deepen student's knowledge, promotes critical thinking and develops independent learning skills.

Issues Online saves precious preparation time. We wade through the wealth of material on the internet to filter the best quality, most relevant and up-to-date information you need to start exploring a topic.

Our carefully selected, balanced content presents an overview and insight into each topic from a variety of sources and viewpoints.

Students

Issues Online is designed to support your studies in a broad range of topics, particularly social issues relevant to young people today.

Thousands of articles, statistics and infographs instantly available to help you with research and assignments.

With 24/7 access using the powerful Algolia search system, you can find relevant information quickly, easily and safely anytime from your laptop, tablet or smartphone, in class or at home.

Visit issuesonline.co.uk to find out more!

Chapter 1

Censorship in the UK

Censorship in the United Kingdom: is it a problem?

By Theodor Porutiu

Almost 100% of internet users are within range of ADSL connections and a 4G network. Moreover, the 2017 Digital Economy Act ensured that access to a broadband connection with a minimum speed of 10 Megabytes per second (Mbps) is effectively a legal right in the UK.

The UK offers relatively unrestricted access to internet content. The filtering and blocking that is in place, is there to remove illegal materials, such as copyrighted media, and child pornography. Moreover, they try to prevent minors from accessing pornographic materials.

There is little to no evidence of politically motivated censorship by the UK government. However, in the wake of several high-profile terrorist attacks, the UK Parliament passed the controversial Investigatory Powers Act, which significantly upgraded law enforcement's ability to conduct surveillance and data collection, even on individuals not suspected of committing a crime.

In this article, we will look at what powers the UK government has to censor the internet, how they use them, and what effect the Investigatory Powers Act has on internet privacy.

What content does the UK government censor?

The UK government usually doesn't get involved in the type of content that people share on the internet. They do have some interesting legal quirks, like how no content can depict their Parliament houses satirically, but generally people can share content freely on the internet if they live in the UK. However, the UK government does censor pornography, terrorism propaganda and torrenting, so let's get into the details.

Pornography

The Digital Economy Act, which came into force in 2017, contained several provisions which required Internet Service Providers (ISPs) and adult content providers to verify the age of users who are attempting to access online pornography.

The Act has generated controversy because it also includes provisions for the blocking of 'extreme' pornographic material. The standards by which they judge pornographic material 'extreme' were criticized as poorly defined and unevenly applied and drew sharp criticism from civil and female rights activists.

Because the Digital Economy Act requires those attempting access to online pornography to verify their age, most commonly done through providing credit card details, there are concerns that personal data could be leaked or hacked, as was the case for the infidelity site, Ashley Madison.

There is also some concern that owners of multiple high profile pornographic sites, could use age verification data to profile UK customers and sell that data to 3rd parties in a manner similar to Facebook.

Illegal material and terrorist content

ISPs in the UK must block access to any content depicting child sexual abuse and provide parents with an 'unavoidable choice' whether they want to enable parental control filters to regulate the content that their children have access to.

A lot of minors use mobile devices in the UK, so they require all mobile service providers to block access to pornographic content for customers who cannot prove that they are over 18 years of age.

Under the 2006 Terrorism Act, any content which contributes to 'the glorification or promotion of terrorism' is blacklisted by the parental control filters provided by ISPs and is not accessible from publicly funded facilities, such as schools and libraries.

They also require UK ISPs to block any domain or URL that hosts content that infringes on UK copyright regulations. The UK High Court can also order websites and platforms to take down copyrighted material but they are not legally liable for user-hosted content unless they refuse to remove it.

Piracy

The UK has always been way ahead of the world in censoring and blocking torrent sites. For example, the UK government worked with ISPs in 2012 to block access to The Pirate Bay and Kickass Torrents, two famous torrent websites, a full three years before the US took Kickass Torrents down.

This is one way the UK Government limits access to the internet, even if torrenting is not illegal. UK citizens, however, can use a VPN to bypass this regulation, so we'll talk more about VPNs below.

How does the UK government censor the internet?

UK-based ISPs use a content filtering technology known as Cleanfeed. Developed by British Telecom in 2004, Cleanfeed is a hybrid system of IP address blocking and deep packet inspection (DPI) based URL blocking. Cleanfeed operates as a two-stage mechanism that filters out specific internet traffic.

While Cleanfeed bears some similarity to the DPI filtering methods employed by Iran and China, the program complies with European Union regulations on internet privacy because it does not enable a 'detailed, invasive analysis of the contents of a data packet.'

The UK Government also cooperates with social media platforms to remove hate speech of any kind, which is, in theory, an infringement on free speech, but it's a well-planned system that protects the disenfranchised from harm online.

On another positive note, the UK government also works closely with civic groups to maintain freedom of speech online. For example, they tried to pass a law in 2006 that would make it illegal to offend someone based on their religious beliefs. However, when both religious organizations and secular NGOs fought against it, the bill was repealed and changed to protect free speech.

Terrorist propaganda

The 2006 Terrorism Act mandates the removal of online material that glorifies or praises terrorism, could be of use to terrorists, or in any way incites individuals to carry out or support terrorist acts.

To investigate internet materials hosted in the UK and oversee the removal of any instances of 'jihadist propaganda,' the UK government set up the Counter Terrorism Internet Referral Unit (CTIRU) in 2010.

CTIRU creates a blacklist of URLs hosting terrorist material outside of the UK and passes it on to service providers to be included in their optional parental filtering. In 2015, the UK Home Secretary reported CTIRU was taking down 'about 1,000 pieces of terrorist- related material per week.'

Despite the creation of a task force and expanded powers to combat hate speech, law enforcement in the UK continues to struggle to apply the 2006 Terrorism Act, particularly in the cases of content hosted by large, overseas-based, social media platforms.

During several high-profile terrorism trials in 2017 and 2018, the UK police reported that they were unable to convince Facebook, Twitter, and YouTube to remove content that 'consistently promoted jihadist violence and glorified acts of terrorism.'

Website owners and platforms who knowingly host user-generated content promoting terrorism or hate speech, and refuse to remove it when made aware of its existence, can be legally held liable under EU Directive 2000/31/EC (the E-Commerce Directive).

The Investigatory Powers Act

The most significant change to internet freedoms in the United Kingdom over the last decade is the signing into law of The Investigatory Powers Act (IP Act) in 2016. The IP Act allows UK law enforcement and intelligence agencies to collect bulk surveillance data on UK citizens through interception, equipment interference, and data retention.

At the time of its passing, the IP attracted huge criticism from a range of political perspectives and prompted Ewan MacAskill, a journalist for the *Guardian* newspaper, to suggest that the IP Act had given the UK government 'the most sweeping surveillance powers in the western world'.

With the IPA, the UK government jeopardized the integrity of internet users' civil rights. It allows government agencies to surveil anyone, even if they didn't commit a crime. Data can be gathered through a wide range of activities, including 'remote access to computers, to downloading the contents of a mobile phone covertly during a search' and security services are not obligated to inform individuals that their data is being kept.

Legal challenges

In April 2018, an investigation by the UK High Court ruled that several provisions of the Investigatory Powers Act, regarding access to individuals' data, was incompatible with EU law.

The EU forced the UK to amend the legislation by November 2018. On the 31st of October, 2018, they added provisions that increased the threshold of when the government can undergo surveillance, to only target extremely dangerous activity, or actual suspects. Regardless, people in the UK still fear the infrastructure is used for lower-profile cases, so many people use a VPN to circumvent government surveillance.

Is a VPN legal to use in the United Kingdom?

Using a Virtual Private Network (VPN) is one of the best ways to circumvent any ban on internet use, and maintain your anonymity.

Additionally, VPN use is entirely legal in the UK, and many internet users make use of a VPN to ensure their online privacy, especially considering the increased powers of the UK government under the IP Act.

What are the best VPN services to use in the United Kingdom?

If you want to bypass any governmental regulation, or if you're just worried about being surveilled, you can always use a VPN to mask your online activity. Here are the best ones you can find.

ExpressVPN

ExpressVPN's super-fast and stable service is ideal if you are travelling and want to keep your communications secure and have full access to all the content you are used to.

With over 2000 servers worldwide and military-grade encryption, ExpressVPN is precisely what you need to circumvent local content restrictions and make sure that cyber criminals can't access your information online.

Lastly, because ExpressVPN has the extra streaming features, and a lot of reliable servers in western countries, it's the best pick for anyone in the United Kingdom, even if it can be a bit pricier than its alternatives.

NordVPN

If you are looking for a VPN that takes your anonymity as seriously as you do, then look no further than NordVPN. With P2P support for downloading torrents, a vast range of servers in over 54 countries, high-level encryption, a built-in kills switch, and an encrypted chatting service, you don't have to worry about online surveillance, regardless of where you are or what you are doing.

NordVPN also has a 'no log record' policy, meaning your actions are as anonymous as they can be and, because NordVPN is headquartered in Panama, they are under no legal obligation to share your details with anyone, ideal if you are worried about being spied on under UK's surveillance operations.

CyberGhost

If you have never used VPNs before, then CyberGhost is an excellent choice. Their system makes use of easy to use and easy to install software and combines it with a user-friendly interface. They aim to make your VPN experience simple and enjoyable.

Final thoughts

By comparison to other countries, the United Kingdom puts very few restrictions on the online content its citizens can access and, until recently, took little action to police their online activities.

However, with introducing the IP Act, in reaction to an increased number of terrorist attacks, the UK government's ability to conduct online surveillance, collect, and keep user's data has grown.

This has led to concern amongst civil liberties groups about how collected data is kept and used, and the ramifications of the government being able to collect data on individuals with no apparent justification. It was repealed, thanks to the EU stepping in, but if you still want to make sure you're not under surveillance, a VPN will rid you of any worry.

FAQ On United Kingdom's Censorship

Below, we answered some frequently asked questions about UK's censorship efforts, like what they're focused on, why, and how to circumvent the government's internet regulations.

Key Facts

- The Digital Economy Act came into force in 2017.
- Investigatory Powers Act was signed into law in 2016. This act allows UK law enforcement and intelligence agencies ability to collect bulk surveillance information on UK citizens through interception, equipment interference and data retention, even on individuals not suspected of committing a crime.
- In 2018 the EU forced the UK to amend provisions in the IPA to limit surveillance, only targeting extremely dangerous activity or actual suspects.
- Using a Virtual Private Network (VPN) is entirely legal in the UK.

Why does the United Kingdom censor the internet?

For the most part, the United Kingdom censors illegal or potentially harmful content, like terrorist propaganda or child pornography. Access to torrent sites is also restricted, even if torrenting in and of itself is not illegal. The reasoning seems sound for all of these actions. The government just wants to protect the population.

However, the UK also runs massive surveillance operations, which exist to keep tabs on its population.

How does the UK censor the internet?

The UK censors the internet through content takedowns, site bans, and most importantly – surveillance mandated by the IP act. It's not an extremely complex censorship system, which is why UK citizens can keep their privacy secure with a VPN. If you're wondering what VPN to use, ExpressVPN is a good choice for UK citizens, because it gives unrestricted access to servers all across the globe, extra features for streaming, and reliable anonymity.

How do I get around internet censorship in the UK?

The best way to circumvent internet censorship in any country is by using a Virtual Private Network. A VPN routes your traffic through servers anywhere on the globe, which changes your IP and maintains your online anonymity. On top, using a VPN also means gaining access to regionally blocked content, like shows on your favourite streaming services.

12 October 2022

Theodor Porutiu, Author
Tech writer
Theodor is a content writer passionate about the newest tech developments and content marketing strategies. He likes privacy-friendly software, SEO tools, and when he's not writing, he's trying to convince people they should uninstall TikTok.

The above information is reprinted with kind permission from vpnoverview.
© 2014-2023 VPNoverview.com

www.vpnoverview.com

The UK risks becoming a world leader in online censorship

By Mark Johnson, Legal and Policy Officer at Big Brother Watch

The emergence of a free and open internet was one of the greatest achievements of liberal democracies. The creation of a decentralised web allowed ordinary citizens in countries all over the world to share and receive information. Now, fears about crime and moral panics about disinformation mean that many liberal democracies are making the web a smaller place for everyone.

On Wednesday, the Government published its Online Safety Bill, a piece of legislation designed to make the UK 'the safest place in the world to go online, and the best place to start and grow a digital business.' Omitted from this description is that the proposed Bill would also make the UK a world leader amongst democracies when it comes to censorship and state control.

The legislation forces large social media companies to act on any content which risks 'having, or indirectly having, a significant adverse physical or psychological impact on an adult.' Such a vague duty will no doubt lead to sites doubling down on controversial or offensive views, which have always been protected as an inherent part of freedom of speech. With a threat of penalties for a failure to remove posts of this nature, online platforms will be forced to snoop on users more and will be quicker to take content down. An entrenchment of surveillance capitalism beckons, only this Bill would make it state backed.

One particularly pernicious element of the wider proposals is the government's intention to clamp down on what they refer to as 'misinformation' and 'disinformation' online – terms undefined in the Bill. How such concepts could be accurately defined and restricted without censoring the lawful expression of internet users is not clear. Over the course of the last year, posts by academics on Facebook or Twitter which have questioned the efficacy of masks have fallen foul of the platforms' broad rules on misinformation. The Online Safety Bill will make this worse and the clear risks to free discussion are obvious.

Amongst other things, the pandemic was a security crisis and many governments around the world, including here in the UK, have begun to develop a growing paranoia about the spread of information they cannot control. Where journalists and politicians once acted as the gatekeepers of expression, the internet has democratised speech and has meant that everyone now has access to a platform. Unfortunately, those in power often do not like this direction of travel.

Curiously, the Online Safety Bill creates carveouts for 'journalistic content' and 'democratic content'. The definition of these concepts remains fuzzy, but what is clear is that these exemptions from the scope of the Bill are designed to give special protection to journalists and politicians; restoring the old gatekeepers of speech whilst bestowing upon the rest of us an online regime of restrictions and censorship. There is no doubt that the media plays a fundamental role in any democracy, yet the question remains: if this legislation does not inhibit free expression as the government claims, why are carveouts for journalists and politicians necessary at all?

This really matters, not just for internet users here in the UK but also for people all around the world. If the United Kingdom creates an online regime which is intolerant of free expression, what is there to stop other, less liberal governments abroad citing British legislation to justify their own censorship?

The willingness of national governments to act as an arbiter of online speech is growing. Only two weeks ago the Indian government, led by Narendra Modi, leant on Twitter to take down tweets which were critical of its pandemic response. And a few months ago, in a brazen act of censorship, they demanded the platform suspend hundreds of accounts which had posted content about the country's farming protests. This collusion between governments and social media giants in the largest democracy in the world should be a warning to anyone who believes in the right to freedom of speech. It is time to push back.

The publication of the draft Online Safety Bill marks the start of its journey through Parliament, but this is just another chapter in a long running conversation about our deteriorating relationship with free speech.

The UK has often been a world leader in promoting human rights and the rule of law, yet this legislation could set a precedent for all of the wrong reasons; introducing state-backed censorship and monitoring on a scale never seen before in the Western world. Parliament must step in to safeguard our right to free expression by removing provisions that restrict lawful speech from the Bill entirely. If it fails to, Britain will only embolden those around the world who would prefer to silence dissenting voices than let them be heard. The future of the free, fair and open internet could depend on it.

14 May 2021

The above information is reprinted with kind permission from Big Brother Watch & *The Spectator*.
© 2023 The Spectator.

www.bigbrotherwatch.org.uk
www.spectator.co.uk

UK government ties itself in knots over social media censorship

The UK government wants to protect us from online horridness but seems confused about how best to go about it while also protecting freedom of speech.

By Scott Bicheno

A parliamentary committee has published a report in to government digital censorship proposals contained in the draft Online Safety Bill. The report is titled *Free for all? Freedom of expression in the digital age* and seems to be positioned as opposition to parts of the Bill. It contains a few mild statements of concern about censorship not always being an unconditionally good thing, while conceding that horridness is bad and must therefore be stamped out with the full force of the law.

One rare substantial critique concerns 'clause 11', which apparently seeks to force internet platforms to stamp out online speech that, while not illegal, is still 'harmful'. 'We do not support the government's proposed duties on platforms in clause 11 of the draft Online Safety Bill relating to content which is legal but may be harmful to adults,' says the summary of the report.

'We are not convinced that they are workable or could be implemented without unjustifiable and unprecedented interference in freedom of expression. If a type of content is seriously harmful, it should be defined and criminalised through primary legislation. It would be more effective–and more consistent with the value which has historically been attached to freedom of expression in the UK–to address content which is legal but some may find distressing through strong regulation of the design of platforms, digital citizenship education, and competition regulation.'

In terms of due process that statement is spot on but it still sidesteps the more fundamental issues surrounding censorship such as enforcement, subjectivity and even desirability. How do we determine whether a type of content is 'seriously harmful', especially since both terms are largely subjective? Are there degrees of harm or just a simple threshold and what is an appropriate and useful punishment for people who cross it? What about context, satire, parody, etc? Even the 'strong regulation of the design of platforms' seems impossible to specify, let alone enforce.

'If the government believes that a type of content is sufficiently harmful, it should be criminalised,' said Lord Gilbert, Chair of the committee. 'We would expect this to include, for example, any of the vile racist abuse directed at members of the England football team which isn't already illegal. It has no place in our society and the full force of the law must be brought down on the perpetrators urgently.'

But it already has, m'lud, with the five UK citizens they were able to identify as responsible for such stuff arrested within days. Civil society is united in condemnation of such abuse, such that 'vile' has now become the obligatory adjective for it, but surely such vileness is not restricted to the culmination of major football tournaments. What about all the other abuse, racist or otherwise, sent to people, footballers or otherwise, constantly on the internet. Should every such case result in an arrest?

Gilbert, sadly, seems to have fallen prey to exactly the kind of policy-by-Twitter that afflicts the government. There was a moral panic following what turned out to be a small number of trolls (yes, even those are too many), most of whom weren't even UK based, such that for several days being seen to respond robustly became the overriding priority of this administration. Meanwhile other, seemingly more malicious, forms of online abuse apparently continue to escape its attention.

'The right to speak your mind is the hallmark of a free society and a right long treasured in Britain but it isn't an unfettered right,' said Gilbert. 'The rights and preferences of individuals must be at the heart of a new, joined-up regulatory approach, bringing together competition policy, data, design, law enforcement and the protection of children. Britain can be a world leader, setting standards to which other countries can aspire. We must get this right.'

Not horrid individuals who say vile things though, eh? Their rights should be fettered and preferences denounced. The report laments the lack of choice in the online platform market and makes vague calls for the internet giants to hand over some money to the police 'on the basis that polluters should pay'. But if the platforms, rather than the individuals that use them, are the polluters, shouldn't it instead be them that become criminalised?

It's all a complete mess. The report's criticisms of the Online Safety Bill are sound, but its proposed remedies are incoherent, insubstantial and inconclusive. Of course there has to be some legal upper limit for speech but that already exists. Lowering that limit in a bid to prevent people saying unpleasant things is not only futile, it would almost certainly cause more harm, via the prevention of free speech and criminalisation of much of the population, than it would prevent.

22 July 2021

Consider

As a class, compile a list of what you deem to be 'seriously harmful content'. Consider whether or not you think some, or all of this content should be criminalised.

The above information is reprinted with kind permission from Telecoms.com
© 2023 Informa PLC.

www.telecoms.com

New UK 'bill of rights' exempts government from free speech protections

Government policies to crack down on protest and other speech exempted from new laws.

By Jon Stone, Policy Correspondent

Boris Johnson's new 'bill of rights' exempts the government itself from having to comply with its new free speech protections, legal experts have warned.

Justice secretary Dominic Raab said last week that the new charter would stop free speech from being 'whittled away' by 'wokery and political correctness'.

But clauses included in the bill specifically exempt laws created by ministers from its new free speech test – meaning it will not protect people from the 'various threats to free speech posed by the government'.

Campaigners said the bill of rights would 'end up hampering efforts to hold the government to account'.

One senior law professor told The Independent that the carve-out was 'very, very odd' because bills of rights around the world, such as in the United States, tend to also apply to the government.

'I think Americans, for example, would just be incredulous – you have a special extra right of free speech, but not against the government,' Gavin Phillipson, professor of law at the University of Bristol, said.

Prof Phillipson, who is also a visiting fellow at the University of Oxford and an authority in comparative free speech law, added: 'They're saying, you have these really strong protections for free speech – except against the government.

'Generally if you look at most threats to free speech, and what most bills of rights around the world are concerned with, it's the various threats to free speech posed by the government. That's very, very odd.

'The fact that the government feels it necessary to exempt a whole range of things it does – particularly the thing people most worry about, being "prosecuted for what you say" – is a very odd look in what's meant to be a bill of rights.'

Clause 4 of the new bill states that 'when determining a question which has arisen in connection with the right to freedom of speech, a court must give great weight to the importance of protecting the right' – a measure meant to generally beef up free speech in judicial decisions.

But Clause 4 (3) says this section 'does not apply' in criminal proceedings or 'of any question whether a provision of primary or subordinate legislation that creates a criminal offence is incompatible with a Convention right'.

This means that offences created by the government cannot be held to be incompatible with the right to free speech under the bill, even if they restrict someone's right to freedom of expression.

The Ministry of Justice denied the approach was a 'carve-out' for ministers and said it was necessary to stop free speech from being 'abused'.

Other parts of the bill also narrow the definition of free speech in a way that appears to exclude some types of protest, by defining it as imparting 'ideas, opinions or information by means of speech, writing or image'.

'They actually restrict the definition of expression to which this applies to only that involving words or images,' Prof Phillipson said.

'There were cases involving hunt saboteurs – direct action protest – that the ECHR [European Court on Human Rights] has held do count as expression.'

He said that the 'restrictive definition of expression must be there to make sure that the various forms of direct action protest that involve more than just chanting slogans and waving banners don't even fall within this clause at all'.

'Where people committed the new public order offences, those would be exempt from this clause anyway, but I think that definition is to make sure that the new police powers in the Public Order Bill can be used against them.'

While claiming to be protecting free speech with the new bill of rights, the government has simultaneously pushed through new authoritarian legislation that cracks down on protest in its Police, Crime, Sentencing and Courts Act.

New police powers came into effect this week and were used to confiscate speakers and amplifiers from long-running anti-Brexit protesters outside parliament – causing an outcry.

The exemption clauses in the bill mean that the new free speech powers would not protect people from being prosecuted for offences such as glorifying terrorism or publishing an image that arouses reasonable suspicion of being a supporter of a proscribed organisation.

'These are the kind of things that under the US first amendment, for example, would be just categorically unconstitutional, and that wouldn't even be a hard case,' Prof Phillipson told *The Independent*.

There are also specific carve-outs in other clauses so the government can ban someone from entering the UK on the basis of what they have said, and protect the home secretary's powers to strip people of their citizenship.

Charlie Whelton, policy and campaigns officer at the human rights group Liberty, said: 'As well as the Rights Removal Bill weakening all of our other rights, it will weaken our right to free speech too.

'The government is falsely claiming they will improve protection for freedom of expression, but this is not true. Clause 4, which directs courts to give "great weight" to the importance of free speech, restricts itself from applying to criminal proceedings, determinations of whether legislation is compatible with human rights, or questions of confidentiality, immigration, citizenship, or national security. The government is making it so that free speech is only valued when it is not used against the government.

'This clause will not protect protesters or whistleblowers, nor will it allow courts to keep a check on the government infringing our free speech rights. Alongside the Policing Act, the Public Order Bill, the Online Safety Bill and more, this is characteristic of a government that claims to protect free speech but wants only to avoid accountability wherever it can.'

A spokesperson for the organisation Index on Censorship also criticised the bill, stating: 'We categorically disagree with the government's claim that the bill will strengthen freedom of expression.

'We believe the bill will only serve to expand state power and will end up hampering efforts to hold the government to account, not least of all around issues relating to national security and citizenship, as mentioned specifically in section 4 of the bill.

'These are issues that are of huge public interest. We must ensure that the necessary checks and balances are in place in order to protect our democracy and our fundamental civil liberties.'

Ministers have generally characterised culture war issues, such as speakers not being invited to universities, as 'free speech' questions, but these have little to do with the legal right to free speech as generally enforced around the world.

'Actually if you think about the major instances of cancel culture they're not usually legal instances, they're people being shamed on Twitter or no-platformed,' said Prof Phillipson.

'In the instances of people being sacked from their jobs, or formally disciplined, they've mainly won their cases. This is a cultural phenomenon really, not a legal one. Universities disinviting speakers because students think they're offensive and so on – these are not infringements of their legal right to free speech because you don't have a right to a particular platform.'

He added: 'The notion that this clause is aimed at combatting "wokery" doesn't make sense to me and suggests that it's more rhetoric aimed at pleasing their supporters and elements, perhaps, of the right-wing press. Because a lot of what the government would think of as cancel culture or "wokery" is not actually to do with the law at all, it's cultural stuff.'

A Ministry of Justice spokesperson said: 'The Bill of Rights strengthens freedom of speech but rightly provides for a limited number of exceptions, such as maintaining a patient's rights to confidentiality or where a criminal act takes place, for example, a hate crime. These exceptions apply to all – they are not a carve-out for government.'

3 July 2022

> **Discuss**
>
> After reading this article, get into pairs and discuss why various organisations advocating for free speech and human rights are against the 'Bill of Rights' being proposed by the current government.

The above information is reprinted with kind permission from *The Independent*.
© independent.co.uk 2023

www.independent.co.uk

How 17th-century Britain's 'cancel culture' can help us understand the importance of free speech

An article from The Conversation.

By Dan Taylor, Lecturer in Social and Political Thought, The Open University and Ariel Hessayon, Reader in early modern History, Goldsmiths, University of London

Free speech is the right to express one's opinions without censorship or restraint. It is a cornerstone of modern liberal democracies. Nowadays, it is considered a basic right in the UN's 1948 Declaration of Human Rights and it is is enshrined in British law.

Yet, free speech is neither historically well established nor widespread.

In many parts of the world, authoritarian governments have prevented citizens' rights to free speech through censorship, mass detentions, surveillance and harassment. At the same time, within liberal democracies there has been growing concern about the overreach of cancelling or no-platforming those with controversial views.

Arguments against free speech have been made for centuries. In 17th-century England, saying or writing something blasphemous would have got your tongue bored through with a red-hot iron. That is what happened to the Quaker James Nayler in 1656.

Nayler engaged in a calculated provocation. He imitated Jesus Christ during a time when many of his religious contemporaries thought that the world was about to end. Other than having his tongue pierced, he was whipped through the streets of London and had his forehead branded with the letter 'B' for good measure.

Seventeenth-century England was a country in crisis. For this was a time of fear, superstition, unaccountable monarchs, wars, religious strife, natural disasters, and the so-called 'Little Ice Age' that severely impacted food production and transportation networks.

As well as the struggles between King Charles I and parliament, there were also rebellions in Scotland and Ireland, all of which were responsible for sparking the civil wars that took place throughout the British Isles.

There were also specific attacks on free speech. In particular, Parliament reimposed press licensing in June 1643. Essentially this system enabled specially appointed officials to suppress inflammatory texts prior to publication or else tone down controversial content.

It was amid these events that poet and polemicist John Milton wrote *Areopagitica* (1644). Here, he argued that press censorship was a mark of tyranny and that, despite persecution, truth would eventually prevail.

Another influential figure at the time was the Dutch philosopher Baruch Spinoza. For Spinoza, there were two key arguments for the right to free speech.

First, by allowing ideas and viewpoints to proliferate, societies and governments can make better decisions that are more representative of the common good. And second, speech and thought can never be truly controlled anyway. Any regime that attempts to bully and control the minds of citizens only ends up inciting resentment and rebellion.

Both Milton and Spinoza were writing in societies marked by varying degrees of censorship and surveillance. Taken together, their ideas would directly influence the

Enlightenment. We may not like everything that we hear or read, they argued, but societies are stronger when the speech of one and all is protected.

Burning books

When Milton published *Areopagitica*, no one had been burned at the stake for heresy in England for more than 30 years. What remained, however, were public book burnings. These mass public displays can be thought of as Protestant Autos da Fé – or ritual displays of humiliation that functioned as a form of purification. They were seen by some contemporaries as echoing an aspect of the terror practised by the Inquisition that operated in several predominantly Catholic areas (a judicial institution established to eradicate heresy).

Over 100 different titles were ordered to be burned in 17th-century England, most between the years 1640–1660, when Milton was writing. While ecclesiastical and secular authorities could no longer burn the bodies of convicted blasphemers and rebels, they could still burn their books.

Sadly, this isn't a matter of historical curiosity. Public book burnings are still familiar even in countries supposedly committed to free speech. Just recently, in Tennessee a pastor organised a public book-burning ceremony to combat 'demonic influences' and 'witchcraft'.

More generally, the US has seen a growing desire to ban books deemed difficult or obscene, such as Margaret Atwood's *The Handmaid's Tale* and Art Spiegelman's moving account of the Holocaust, *Maus*. The American Library Association recently reported that it's received an 'unprecedented' rise in requests to ban 'objectionable' books – around 330 books in total.

That free speech is still (though only symbolically) burnt at the stake today points to the enduring challenges presented by difficult, unpopular or repugnant ideas. Suspicion against all types of censorship is a healthy sign that the public is willing and capable to make up their own minds.

Thanks to the likes of Milton and Spinoza, the attacks on free speech of the 17th century eventually gave way to a much more liberal culture in parts of western Europe. Had there not been this reaction to censorship during the early modern period, we wouldn't have had some of the ideas of religious tolerance and democratic participation that went on to underpin the Enlightenment.

15 February 2022

Key Facts

- Free speech is the right to express one's opinions without censorship or restraint.
- Free speech is a basic right in the UN's 1948 Declaration of Human Rights and it is enshrined in British law.
- In 17th-century Etngland, saying something blasphemous would have got your tongue bored through with a red-hot iron.
- Over 100 different titles were ordered to be burned in 17th-century England, most between the years 1640–1660, when John Milton was writing.
- The American Library Association recently reported that it's received an 'unprecedented' rise in requests to ban 'objectionable' books – around 330 books in total.

THE CONVERSATION

The above information is reprinted with kind permission from The Conversation.
© 2010-2023, The Conversation Trust (UK) Limited

www.theconversation.com

Cancel culture: what views are Britons afraid to express?

Those with less progressive views on divisive social topics feel more reluctant to voice their opinion.

By Matthew Smith, Head of Data Journalism

One of the new political catchphrases of recent years has been 'cancel culture'. As with so many Westminster Bubble terms, it is an import from the United States, and refers to a desire or attempts to ostracise (or 'cancel') people or organisations with certain viewpoints, generally those that are considered un-progressive.

As we found with our earlier study on another American political import – being 'woke' – Britons don't know what the political elite are on about when they bring up cancel culture.

Only a third of Britons (35%) say they think they know what cancel culture means. Almost two thirds don't know what it means (65%), including close to four in ten who've never heard the expression in the first place (38%).

Young people are more familiar with cancel culture, with 45% of 18-24 year olds saying they know what it is, compared to 40% of 25-49 year olds, 31% of 50-64 year olds, and 26% of those aged 65 and above.

In fact, approaching half of 65+ year olds have never heard the term used in the first place (45%), twice as many as 18-24 year olds (23%).

While most Britons aren't familiar with 'cancel culture' as a phrase, that's not to say Britons don't feel 'cancelled' from time to time.

A majority of Britons (57%) say they have, at least sometimes, found themselves stopping themselves from expressing their political or social views for fear of judgement or negative responses from others.

Conservative voters are more likely to say so than Labour voters (68% vs 53%), although notably most people in both groups feel this way. Women are also more likely to have held their tongue than men (62% vs 52%).

Only a quarter of Britons (27%) say they always express their political or social views if they want to do so, regardless of potential judgement.

When have people kept quiet about their views?

This is not to suggest that any example of someone holding back is an example of cancel culture. Asked in what circumstances people have kept their lips zipped, Britons are most likely to do so with people they've only just met (49%), perhaps an understandable occasion on which to avoid a potential argument.

Likewise, four in ten Britons (40%) have done so at work, while one in three (34%) have avoided speaking their mind on social media, 31% have done so among friends, and 21% while with their family.

Most Britons say that at least sometimes they feel unable to express their political or social views for fear of judgement or negative responses

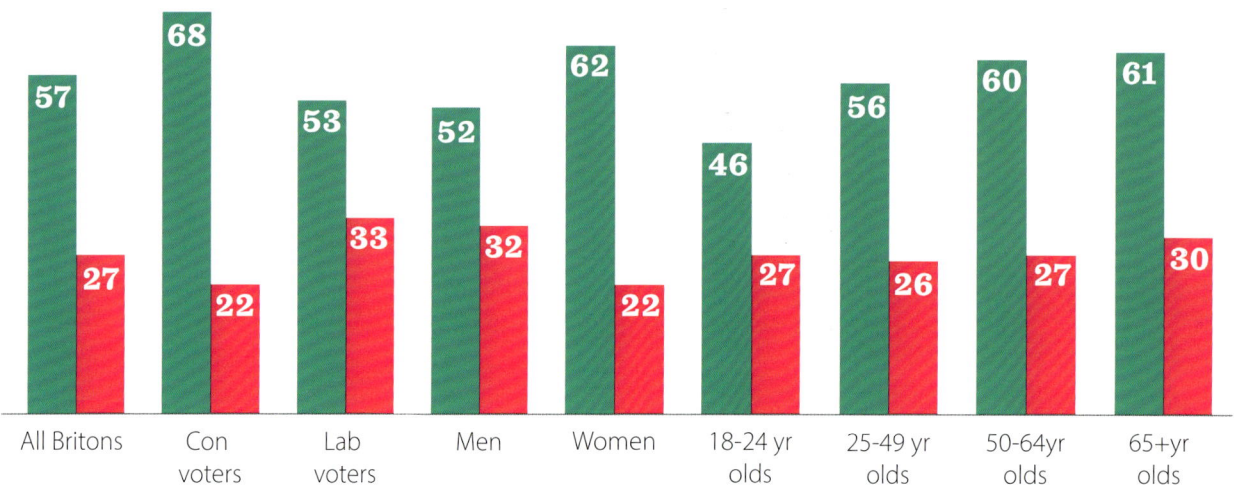

Source: YouGov

Thinking specifically about when the following topics come up, how often, if at all, do you find yourself stopping yourself from expressing your views for fear of judgement or negative responses from others?

% of those holding each view who say 'always' or 'most times'

Topic: Immigration levels to the UK

View: Generally speaking, immigration into Britain has been a bad thing for the country — 33

View: Generally speaking, immigration into Britain has been a good thing for the country — 10

Topic: Race relations and discrimination against ethnic minorities

View: British people from ethnic minorites have things just as good in the UK as white Britons — 31

View: British people from ethnic minorites still face significant discrimination and disadvantages compared to white Britons — 11

Topic: Transgender issues

View: I disagree with the statement 'a transgender woman is a woman' — 29

View: I agree with the statement 'a transgender woman is a woman' — 10

Topic: Islamic religious beliefs and practices

View: A law against wearing full body and face veils (like burqas and niqabs) should be introduced — 28

View: People should be allowed to decide for themselves what to wear (including burqas and niqabs) — 11

Topic: Sexuality and gay rights issues

View: Gay, lesbian and bisexual people in the UK have things just as good as straight people — 21

View: Gay, lesbian and bisexual people still face significant discrimination and disadvantages in the UK compared to straight people — 10

Topic: Gender and women's rights issues

View: Women in the UK have things just as good as men — 20

View: Women still face significant discrimination and disadvantages in the UK compared to men — 13

Topic: Britain's past and the British Empire

View: Britain's past is something we should be more proud of — 15

View: Britain's past is something we should be more ashamed of — 11

Topic: My views on the Conservative party

View: I could see myself some day voting for the Conservative party — 14

View: I could never see myself voting for the Conservative party — 13

Topic: Obesity and the lifestyle choices around it

View: Being overweight is unhealthy and is something that should be discouraged — 13

View: People should be made to feel good about whatever body size or shape they are — 11

Source: YouGov

What views are Britons reluctant to express?

What views do people feel like they can't express? To test this, we asked Britons a series of wedge questions on several divisive topics to see what side of an argument they came down on. Then we asked how often they find themselves hiding their views on those topics for fear of negativity.

In most cases, those holding what might be considered the 'un-progressive' view more frequently omit their opinions on that topic.

For example, those who believe immigration has generally been a bad thing for the UK are more likely to say they always or mostly have to hide their views on the subject of immigration levels to the UK (33%) than those who think immigration has been a good thing for the UK (10%). This

When it comes to the balance between free speech and protecting people from hateful or offensive speech, which do you think should be prioritised more? %

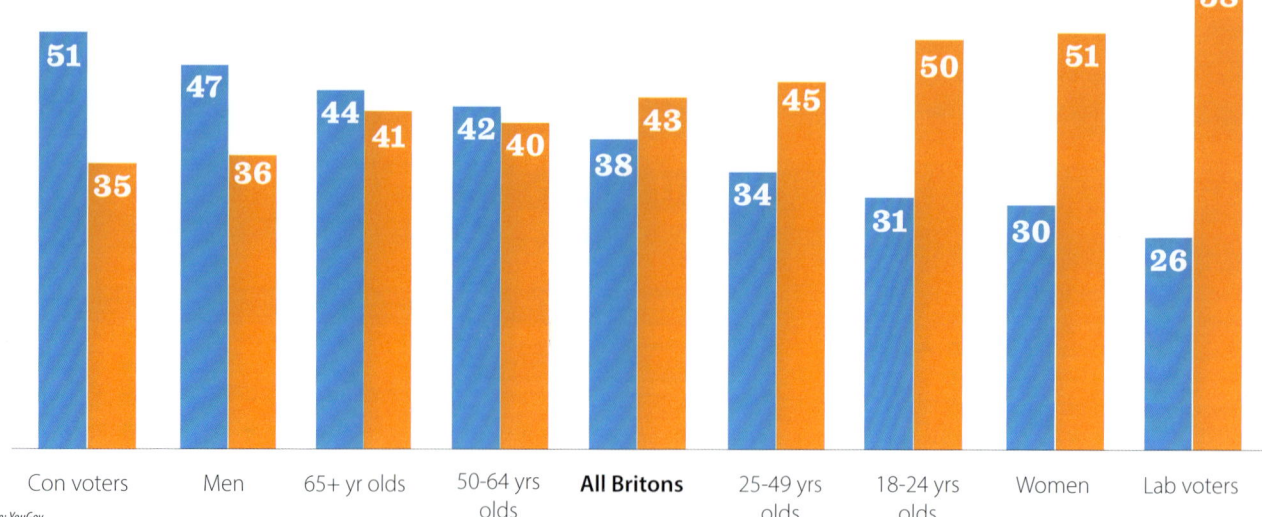

Source: YouGov

is the topic on which people are most likely to say they feel they have to keep quiet.

Other top views people are more reluctant to express are the belief that ethnic minorities in Britain have things as good as white Britons, with 31% who hold this view feel they can't ever or mostly can't say so, and transgender issues, which 29% of those who disagree with the statement 'a transgender woman is a woman' feel they have to frequently keep bottled up.

The exceptions to this trend are views on the British Empire and obesity, where both sides of the argument reported similar levels of reluctance to express themselves. When it came to views on the Conservative party, although there is not much difference at the always/mostly level, those with pro-Tory views are more likely to say they sometimes or rarely have to hide that fact than those with a negative opinion of the party.

Across all nine scenarios, only about 10-14% of those who sit on the more progressive side of the argument say they feel they always/sometimes have to keep their opinion to themselves.

'I used to be with "it", but then they changed what "it" was. Now what I'm with isn't "it" anymore and what's "it" seems weird and scary. It'll happen to you!'

Comedian Ricky Gervais, who has been an outspoken critic of cancel culture, predicted recently that the views that young people hold today will in turn come to be seen as backward by future generations

'I wanna live long enough to see the younger generation not be woke enough for the next generation. It's going to happen. Don't they realise that, it's like, they're next. That's what's funny.'

It seems that, indeed, young people do not expect to become the bad guys. Only one in three 18-24 year olds

(36%) think that some of their current views will come to be seen as unacceptable by future generations of young people during their own lifetime. An equal number (35%) anticipate their own future cancellation, however, while 29% are unsure.

By contrast, almost half of the oldest Britons (47% of those aged 65 and above) expect some of their views to be seen as bad by future youngsters. One in three nevertheless are sure they'll hold acceptable views until they die (35%).

What should we prioritise more: protecting free speech or stopping offensive and hateful speech?

Underpinning the whole cancel culture argument is the dilemma of how far societies should go to preserve free speech when that right is often exercised in ways ranging from the hurtful to the malicious.

Asked which should be the priority, 38% of Britons say the focus should be on protecting free speech, while 43% say protecting people from offensive or hateful speech should be the priority.

Men are much more concerned about protecting free speech and women are more concerned about blocking offensive/hateful speech. Likewise, Tories and Labour voters come down on opposite sides. Younger people are also much more concerned about protecting against offensive/hateful speech than protecting free speech, while older Britons are split between the two.

22 December 2021

The above information is reprinted with kind permission from YouGov.
© 2023 YouGov PLC

www.yougov.co.uk

Free speech 'stifled' as universities cancel record number of speakers

'Deeply worrying trend' emerges as nearly 200 requests for events rejected in a year

By Louisa Clarence-Smith, Education Editor

Freedom of speech is at risk of being stifled on campuses after a record number of speakers and events were rejected last year, the universities watchdog has warned.

The Office for Students found that nearly 200 requests for events and speakers were rejected by English universities and colleges in 2020-21, up from 94 in the previous academic year.

Susan Lapworth, the watchdog's interim chief executive, said she was concerned about the possibility that 'lawful views are being stifled'.

She warned universities that they would face regulatory intervention if they failed to meet their obligations on freedom of speech.

Topics that 'some may find offensive or controversial must be open to free debate' on campuses and across research communities, she said.

'Chilling effect of censorship on campuses'

The vice-chancellor of the University of Essex apologised last year after a seminar on trans rights and the criminal justice system was cancelled following complaints that the speaker was a 'transphobe' who was likely to engage in 'hate speech'.

The university was also criticised after Prof Rosa Freedman, an expert in international human rights law at the University of Reading, was not invited to speak at a seminar on anti-Semitism after concerns were raised about her gender-critical views.

Andrea Jenkyns, the higher education minister, said the watchdog's findings were 'very concerning'.

She said: 'Universities and colleges must be places that champion debate and diversity of thought, and this government has warned of the chilling effect of censorship on our campuses.'

Under proposals in the Higher Education (Freedom of Speech) Bill currently going through Parliament, universities will have a legal duty to actively promote free speech. University governing bodies are currently required to take reasonable steps to ensure that freedom of speech within the law is maintained.

The Office for Students, which has the power to fine or deregister education providers, said it could not confirm whether it has previously penalised any universities over their handling of freedom of speech because it would risk 'prejudicing ongoing enquiries'.

The regulator found that 193 events were rejected out of a total of 19,407 reported to it last year, the highest number recorded since it started collecting data in 2017.

'Tip of the iceberg'

Toby Young, of the Free Speech Union, said: 'This is a deeply worrying trend, but it's just the tip of the iceberg.

'In the past 12 months, the Free Speech Union has helped hundreds of students and academics who've got into trouble for pushing back against ideological orthodoxy on campus, whether it's refusing to do unconscious bias training, criticising their university's links with Stonewall, objecting to the decolonisation of the curriculum, or daring to point out that George Floyd had a criminal record.'

Undergraduates are significantly less supportive of free expression than they were six years ago, according to research by the Higher Education Policy Institute.

The think tank surveyed 1,000 undergraduates and found that 61 per cent say 'when in doubt', their own university 'should ensure all students are protected from discrimination rather than allow unlimited free speech' – up from 37 per cent in 2016.

A spokesman for Universities UK said: 'Institutions do all they can to ensure a culture which encourages free speech and academic freedom so diverse groups and individuals can participate in debate and discussion, with mutual dignity and respect.

'Vice-chancellors support universities playing a more active and visible role in promoting free speech and encouraging debate, and these latest figures show that universities and student unions continue to host tens of thousands of events each year, with less than one per cent not going ahead, often for logistical reasons such as late booking requests.'

14 July 2022

The above information is reprinted with kind permission from The Telegraph.
© Telegraph Media Group Limited 2022

www.telegraph.co.uk

Most students think UK universities protect free speech, survey finds

King's College London finds 65% believe campuses places of 'robust debate' – but growing number disagrees

By Richard Adams, Education Editor

Most UK students say their universities are places of free speech and debate – although a growing number are aware of free speech being restricted on campus, a study published by King's College London has found.

The analysis, by KCL's Policy Institute, found that 65% of students agreed that 'free speech and robust debate are well protected in my university', a higher proportion than the 63% who felt that way in a survey three years ago.

But the survey of 1,500 current students found that one in four had 'often' heard of incidents at their university where free speech had been inhibited, double the 12% who said the same in 2019. And 32% said they had not heard of any incidents, fewer than the 44% in 2019.

Students also displayed hostility towards speakers with offensive views but supported the government's efforts to protect expression and debate on campus through its higher education freedom of speech bill, currently before parliament.

Bobby Duffy, the director of KCL's Policy Institute, said the surveys showed a 'large majority' of students thought universities were protecting free speech, at the same time as increasing minorities of students felt it was under threat.

'While students tend to be a little more sensitive to causing offence than the public, they are not the "snowflakes" they are sometimes made out to be: it's clear that they value free speech, with majorities supportive of measures to bolster it,' Duffy said.

'Universities should have confidence that the starting point on free speech is not as dire as it is sometimes painted but also recognise that it is too important an issue to overlook.

'The government, in turn, need to ensure any measures are applied carefully and proportionately, including looking for positive measures to support free speech, not just regulating against it being curtailed.'

Nearly half the students surveyed thought universities were becoming less tolerant of a wide range of views, with 50% feeling that people with conservative views were reluctant to express them and 36% that those with leftwing views were reluctant to express them.

And 41% of students agreed that academics who taught material that offended students should be fired, while 39% agreed that student unions should ban speakers who could cause offence.

Most students said they knew nothing or very little about the new bill but after it was outlined to them, six in 10 supported it, including 71% who supported universities and student unions having to maintain free speech codes of conduct.

28 September 2022

Research

Have a look at news online (news sites, social media, etc) and see how many stories you can find about UK universities where there are claims that free speech has been restricted. Share your findings with the class.

The above information is reprinted with kind permission from *The Guardian*.
© 2023 Guardian News and Media Limited

www.theguardian.com

Financial censorship

The new front in the war on free speech.

By Freddie Attenborough

> **Write**
>
> Write a short definition of the term 'financial censorship' as you understand it in the context of this article.

The Free Speech Union has been demonetised by US payments company PayPal for daring to stand up for free speech and freedom of expression. PayPal UK, the company whose Twitter banner proudly proclaims that it is 'open for all', has now permanently shut the accounts of the Free Speech Union, as well as the personal account of the organisation's co-founder and General Secretary, Toby Young, and Toby's news website, the Daily Sceptic, without prior warning, meaningful explanation or recourse to a proper appeals process.

So how did we get here – to a world in which a financial intermediary like PayPal can so casually close the account of the Free Speech Union, an organisation set up to defend people's right to free speech, and that does so without taking sides on the issues that those people are speaking about?

The fact is that the relatively recent digitalisation of financial transactions has placed a vast amount of power in the hands of financial services companies like payment processors, banks, online platforms and credit companies like Visa and Mastercard. It is 'FinTech' that now owns and controls the technical, algorithmic means to move virtual money seamlessly around the world in real-time. For a while, the risk that these powers might be exercised to completely cut off and shut up groups, organisations and people seemed entirely abstract. More recently, though, we've seen governments leaning on these companies to act in ways beneficial to state interests.

In 2019, for instance, the Russian government froze bank accounts linked to opposition politician Alexei Navalny (Reuters); in February 2022, Canada froze the bank accounts of the mostly peaceful truckers protesting against the vaccine mandates with no due process, appeals process or court order necessary (*Mail*); then, in early 2022, cross-border payment system SWIFT took the unprecedented move to cut Russia's central bank from its global financial messaging service (*Telegraph*).

But that was all at the behest of governments. What's new is financial services companies like PayPal throwing their weight about and attempting to influence what kind of speech is or isn't acceptable on the basis of their own, decidedly woke corporate values.

Does that mean the withdrawal of financial services from people and organisations that express dissenting opinions on those topics is the new front in the ongoing war against free speech? Sarah McLellan, writing in *Spectator Australia*, certainly thinks so. Citing Jesse Powell, Chief Executive of Kraken Bitcoin Exchange, she argues that 'the traditional financial system has essentially been weaponised' and that losing free access to funding streams on account of one's political views is tantamount to losing free speech.

'PayPal undoubtedly has form.'

PayPal undoubtedly has form in that regard. Earlier this year, *Rolling Stone* contributing editor Matt Taibbi published a story about how the company has been selectively de-platforming alternative media sites that published stories contradicting some of the West's reporting of the Russian

invasion of Ukraine. Among those to have been banned were Mint Press News, a left-wing web-based outlet, and Consortium News, founded by the late Associated Press investigative reporter Robert Parry in 1995 as one of the web's very first independent, reader-funded news outlets.

More recently, we've seen sites that raise perfectly lawful questions about Covid vaccines also getting demonetised by PayPal, including the U.K. Medical Freedom Alliance. (As in Toby's case, Liz Evans, the head of the UKMFA, had her personal PayPal account closed at the same time.) Law-or-fiction, a site run by lawyers and dedicated to helping citizens understand their rights and how they may have been affected as a result of the UK government's response to Covid-19, suffered the same fate a few weeks ago. UsforThem, a parents' group that fought to keep schools open during the pandemic, announced just this week that its account had been shut down by PayPal due to 'the nature of its activities' (Telegraph). And then there's Conservative group Moms for Liberty, and the personal website of gender ideology critic Colin Wright, and... I could go on.

As Matt Taibbi explains, 'going after cash is a big jump from simply deleting speech and actually has a much bigger chilling effect'. This is especially true when it comes to alternative media or grassroots campaigning, where 'money has long been notoriously tight', and the loss of a few thousand pounds here or there can have a major effect on a project, website, podcast or whatever else.

Up until now, companies like PayPal, GoFundMe, Patreon and CrowdJustice have 'only' demonetised individuals and groups whose views they disapprove of. But 'open for all' PayPal has just decided to close the account of the Free Speech Union, an organisation that defends people's right to free speech, without taking sides on the issues they're speaking about.

Is this now the benchmark for all subsequent forms of financial censorship? If so, then as Toby Young pointed out on GB News the night the story broke, PayPal has just significantly – and singlehandedly – 'narrowed the Overton Window', ensuring that 'there are now certain issues you aren't allowed to defend people for expressing sceptical opinions about'.

That's why, as the switch to a cashless society gathers speed, the Government will need to put laws in place to protect people from being punished by companies like PayPal for the expression of dissenting views. But what sorts of laws? 'The challenge,' as Fraser Nelson points out, will be to make the case that 'protecting diversity should also mean diversity of opinion' (Telegraph).

One possible solution to Fraser's 'challenge' was outlined by Toby Young in a comment piece for the Telegraph: passing legislation 'to make it illegal for financial services companies to discriminate against customers on the basis of their political beliefs, provided they're within the law'. The Equality Act 2010 does of course provide some protection in that regard, making it unlawful for companies to discriminate against customers on the basis of their political beliefs (in most circumstances). But like most Big Tech companies, PayPal isn't within scope because it's headquartered in Luxembourg.

A few days after the story broke, it emerged that questions were being raised in governmental circles regarding PayPal's actions, and, just as importantly, the regulatory environment in which companies like PayPal presently operate. According to the Sunday Express, for instance, 'politicians have reacted with fury to PayPal's actions, with one Conservative peer saying she had "never seen so much cross-party outrage" over the move.' The paper went on to note that the financial services company 'faces a political battle, with politicians lining up to call for action against the US company'.

Specifically, dozens of MPs and peers from across the political divide – including 21 Tory MPs and 15 Tory peers as well as four crossbench peers, a Labour peer and a Labour MP – have now written to Business Secretary Jacob Rees-Mogg urging the government to hold PayPal to account. In their letter, the politicians point out that the 'common theme' among the organisations and individuals that have had their accounts closed – the Free Speech Union, Daily Sceptic, Law or Fiction, and UsforThem – is that they are all prominent 'champions of free speech' who have expressed 'critical, non-conforming views on lockdown policies'. Understood in that context, they suggest, it is more than a little difficult 'to avoid construing PayPal's actions as an orchestrated, politically motivated move to silence critical or dissenting views within the UK'.

This is strong stuff, and suggests that there's a real determination across both Houses of Parliament to explore the possibility of developing a legislative mechanism capable of preventing Big Tech companies headquartered outside the UK from censoring people or groups in this country for the expression of legal but dissenting views (or, as in the case of the Free Speech Union, for simply defending those who express legal but dissenting views).

Let's hope our legislators can come up with an effective mechanism sooner rather than later. As we hurtle towards a cashless society, the creeping trend of Big Tech platforms financially censoring groups or individuals who express dissenting views needs to be checked before it starts to become institutionally normalised.

And by the way, the issues at stake here go way beyond the politics of left or right, socialism or liberalism, Labour or Conservative. It doesn't matter who you are or what you believe – financial bullying has no place in a Western liberal democracy.

27 September 2022

The above information is reprinted with kind permission from *The Critic*.
© 2023 Locomotive 6960 Limited

www.thecritic.co.uk

PayPal reinstates Free Speech Union accounts after being accused of 'politically motivated' ban

Payments firm issues statement voicing support for freedom of expression following criticism of freeze by MPs.

By Tony Diver, Whitehall Correspondent and Henry Bodkin, Senior Reporter

PayPal has reinstated the accounts of a free speech campaign group after it was accused by MPs of imposing an 'orchestrated, politically motivated' ban.

The US finance company froze three accounts run by Toby Young, the general secretary of the Free Speech Union (FSU).

The move sparked outrage among MPs, who wrote to Jacob Rees-Mogg, the Business Secretary, and the chairman of the Treasury select committee to urge them to intervene.

On Tuesday night, PayPal said it had decided to reinstate the accounts and issued a statement declaring its support for freedom of expression.

The company also apologised to Mr Young for 'any inconvenience caused' by its investigation, which he said had been a 'nightmare' and would mean he does not use the company again.

Accounts owned by the FSU and the Daily Sceptic blog were frozen on Sept 15 along with an account run by UsForThem, a group that campaigned for schools to reopen during the UK's Covid lockdown.

UsForThem's account was reinstated after an internal review, but the FSU's remained closed until Tuesday. It is understood PayPal had decided the FSU had broken its terms of use but decided to reverse the freeze after it was criticised in the media and by MPs.

Michael Gove and David Davis, both former ministers, Sir Iain Duncan Smith, an ex-Conservative leader, and Sir Graham Brady, the 1922 committee chairman, signed the letter to Mr Rees-Mogg.

They said it was 'hard to avoid construing PayPal's actions as an orchestrated, politically motivated move to silence critical or dissenting views on these topics within the UK'.

A second letter, signed by 41 MPs and peers, was sent to Mel Stride, the chairman of the Treasury Select Committee, on Monday, calling for an investigation and accusing PayPal of issuing 'private economic sanctions' against groups it disagrees with.

Mr Rees-Mogg previously said PayPal should not engage in 'cancel culture', but it is understood there was no direct contact between the company and the Government.

Speaking to *The Telegraph*, Mr Young said: 'Forgive me if I don't leap for joy. The last two weeks have been a nightmare as I've scrabbled to try to stop the Daily Sceptic and Free Speech Union going under. PayPal's software was embedded in all our payment systems, so the sudden closure of our accounts was an existential threat.

'I won't be using PayPal again, at least not until it reinstates all the other people and organisations whose accounts it has closed for political reasons and agrees never to cancel anyone's accounts for purely political reasons again.

'In the meantime, I'm going to be lobbying the Government to change the law so companies like PayPal cannot demonetise people or organisations whose perfectly lawful views it disapproves of.'

The Telegraph understands several Conservative MPs are considering attempting to amend forthcoming legislation to add a ban on payments companies freezing accounts for political reasons.

A PayPal spokesman said: 'PayPal is dedicated to providing safe and affordable financial services to people of all backgrounds with a diversity of views, and we are a strong supporter of freedom of expression and open dialogue.

'We have continued to review the information and we take seriously the input from our customers and stakeholders. Based on these ongoing reviews, we have made the decision to reinstate these accounts. We will continue to work hard to protect freedom of expression, our customers, and our platform.'

27 September 2022

The above information is reprinted with kind permission from *The Telegraph*.
© Telegraph Media Group Limited 2022

www.telegraph.co.uk

Press Freedom

What is free press, and how does it work? What is its role in a democracy?

What does free press mean, how does it work, and what is its role in a modern democracy? We break down its importance, and why it's under threat – even in the EU.

By Jonathan Day

What we read, hear and share every day, whether reading through the daily newspaper in the morning or having a conversation with our friends, forms a central part of our democracy. Getting good information about the society we live in, and then having free and open discussions about how things are and how they should change, is the sort of dialogue that nurtures a strong democracy. And it all depends on having a free press.

What is free press?

When we say a country has a free press, we mean that its news outlets and other publications, even individual citizens, have the right to communicate information without influence or fear of retribution from the state or other powerful entities or individuals. We often use the term 'free press' and 'independent journalism,' a subject we previously explored, more or less interchangeably.

In modern history, a shared understanding of the principle of a free press was outlined by the United Nations in 1948. Article 19 of the Universal Declaration of Human Rights codifies it along with the right free speech:

'Everyone has the right to freedom of opinion and expression; this right includes freedom to hold opinions without interference, and to seek, receive, and impart information and ideas through any media regardless of frontiers.'

Today, most democracies have some protection for a free press, whether this protection comes from a constitution or individual law. In Europe, a free press is protected under Article 10 of the European Convention on Human Rights, and under Article 11 of the EU Charter of Fundamental Rights.

What is the purpose of a free press?

The purpose of a free press is to ensure that the people are free to receive and impart information that is not manipulated or serving a particular person, entity or interest. Its duty, in fact, is often to investigate people of power, and especially the government, to ask the hard questions and to attempt to uncover what's really happening, regardless of the political fallout.

Why is freedom of the press so important?

Simply put, you can't have much of a democracy without a free press. That's because democracy's strength rests in the hands of the people, meaning they have to be knowledgeable and informed in order to make the right decisions when they go to vote.

And then they have to have a fair picture of what happens next – how the elected politicians or other decisions taken with the ballot worked out.

A free press aids in every step of this process. It delivers information to voters before they vote; it fosters dialogue and debate to enrich understanding of this information; and then it reports back to citizens about what their government is doing and if the things they wanted to happen are actually happening. In democracy, citizens delegate decision-making power to their elected officials, and a free press is one way to check on them.

What is (or should be) the role of a free press in a democracy?

A free press is a vital organ of a democratic society. In order for us to make informed choices when we pick our representatives or vote on certain issues, we need to know what's actually going on. A free press can give us the straight story on issues, policies and events because it's not under the influence of the government or the prime minister's golf buddies.

Another function of a free press is that of a watchdog. As it's not beholden to the government or other entity, or working in fear of them, a free press can give unvarnished reporting on politicians and others. Corruption, patronage, embezzlement, a quite regrettable weekend in Ibiza – it's often the case that we learn of misdeeds by our representatives or other authorities only thanks to a society that protects freedom of the press.

And, of course, we want to discuss all this. A free press helps us do that. It creates more opportunities for us to hear other viewpoints or new information, and gives each of us the chance to impart our own opinions and understandings to others. The more we discuss things, the better informed we become and the better able we are to make the best decisions about our future.

Are there legal limits of free press around the world?

Even in countries with a strong tradition of free press and a saturated, diverse media market, there are limits to what a journalist or newspaper or TV anchor can report. For example, journalists aren't free to report on issues that might compromise national security or reveal state secrets.

But perhaps a better way to look at this is by assessing undue limits placed on free press. It's restricted in many countries – North Korea has no free press whatsoever, and doesn't try all that hard to pretend otherwise; Hungary pretends to have free press and is even legally bound to protect it, but now it has only a handful of independent media outlets.

As noted, EU law compels EU member states to protect freedom of the press. And very many of them do, supporting rich and robust media environments that stand as examples for so many other countries around the world. But Hungary is not alone among those EU members that flout this basic right.

In Poland, a state-run oil company bought up one of the largest media groups in the country, Polska Press, last year. With an audience of some 17 million, of a total Polish population of some 38 million, the state now has the ability to heavily control the news that nearly half the country consumes. And a priest who is very close with the government owns one of the other leading media companies, extending the government's reach further still.

In the Czech Republic, Prime Minister Andrej Babiš owns a huge swathe of the country's media outlets. A 2015 report by Foreign Policy said he uses these to 'regularly feature sympathetic coverage' of himself – and 'criticism of his opponents.' In Slovenia, the government is actively weakening the free press. A recent report found that Slovenia 'has seen press freedom deteriorate ever since [Prime Minister Janez] Jansa returned to power in March 2020.'

But the deterioration of the free press is becoming a global phenomenon. The 2021 Reporters Without Borders report on world press freedom finds a worsening state of free press almost everywhere. Disturbingly, it appears that this drop is at least in part related to the COVID-19 pandemic, as nearly 75% of countries to some degree blocked free media during the pandemic.

Why is free press declining?

Free press is under threat or declining precisely because it is so important to democracy. Authoritarian governments want to retain power above all else. That they are so often incredibly corrupt, if not also incompetent, would probably threaten their grip on power, assuming the citizens are given the truth. But when there is no free press, when the stream of information is controlled by the government or oligarchs, the people are given a distorted picture of what's happening.

It's also in decline because the media landscape has changed. Facebook, Google and other Big Tech companies have carved out such a position of market dominance that it is very hard for smaller companies, for independent news outlets or other publications, to compete. These platforms aggregate news and share it with their users, with little to no revenue flowing back to the source that actually wrote the news. This regime must change if we are to protect the plurality and diversity of our media landscape and maintain a truly free press.

What can we do to increase free press?

If we are fortunate enough to live in a country with a free press, we should support it. Supporting free media can be done through donations, by participating in debates, reading newspapers, and teaching kids and the elderly how to use online media safely and without getting lost in the flow of disinformation. It also means we support the right to free speech, which goes hand in hand with having a free press. And we can vote for politicians that support these things as well, in the hope that they can legislate to protect the free press, for instance by regulating the advertising industry or digital media so as to give small, independent outlets a chance to compete with Big Tech.

9 November 2021

Key Facts

- In Europe a free press is protected under Article 10 of the European Convention on Human Rights, and under Article 11 of the EU Charter of Fundamental Rights.

- Press freedom is restricted in many countries – North Korea has no free press whatsoever, and doesn't try all that hard to pretend otherwise; Hungary pretends to have free press and is even legally bound to protect it, but now it has only a handful of independent media outlets.

- The 2021 Reporters Without Borders report on world press freedom finds a worsening state of free press almost everywhere. Disturbingly, it appears that this drop is at least in part related to the COVID-19 pandemic, as nearly 75% of countries to some degree blocked free media during the pandemic.

The above information is reprinted with kind permission from LIBERTIES
© 2023 Civil Liberties Union for Europe

www.liberties.eu

European Parliament appears to censor report on press censorship in EU

The European Parliament removed a reference to Greece's low ranking on the *Press Freedom Index*.

By Yiannis Baboulias

The European Parliament has told *Byline Times* that it removed an article from its website about a report raising concerns around press freedom and censorship in the EU as a whole and Greece in particular as 'it was not in line with editorial guidelines'.

The latest *Press Freedom Index* by Reporters Without Borders ranked Greece last in the EU on the issue – below Malta, Hungary and Bulgaria.

Given that Reporters Without Borders is an official partner of the European Parliament, an article expressing concern over the ranking was posted on the Parliament's website and tweets about it were shared on Twitter.

But then, less than 48 hours later, the article and tweets had disappeared – with no explanation given as to why. It seemed that a discussion concerning censorship and threats to freedom of speech in the EU was itself censored.

A new article was then posted on the European Parliament's website – this time not mentioning the report and its findings at all, but expressing general concern and including a link to the Press Freedom Index near the bottom of the web page.

The European Parliament told *Byline Times*: 'The online article on Reporters Without Borders' world press freedom report was withdrawn from the website as it was not in line with the editorial guidelines for Parliament's communication services. According to these guidelines, editorial products should always mention a clear link to Parliament's activities and agenda, which was not the case here.'

Despite this, similar reports by Reporters Without Borders are still on the European Parliament's website and have not faced similar issues.

On the surface, this incident may seem trivial. But it is just one side of a worsening situation. And the problem goes well beyond freedom to publish – it is about corruption, violence and death at the EU's borders.

A chilling effect

The *Press Freedom Index* naturally rattled the Greek Government. Prime Minister Kyriakos Mitsotakis, who likes to present himself as a liberal reformer, disputed its methodology.

Mitsotakis and his spokespeople have referred to Reporters Without Borders as a 'leftist French NGO' – a term which they have been using to dismiss damning reports by NGOs on Greece's much-criticised treatment of refugees crossing into the country from Turkey.

It has become a standard way for the ruling party to deflect, not only from well-covered reports of illegal pushbacks in the Aegean and in the Evros river, but also reports of police violence against civilians and journalists – and generally any story that might present the Government in a bad light.

Greek journalists are used to this kind of treatment. The Government, through a network of friendly businessmen, has almost complete control of the mainstream press.

Having brought the state media under the direct control of the Prime Minister's office and installed cadres in management, the Government's grip on the message is almost absolute. Journalists investigating illegal push-backs or other scandals find themselves under surveillance or face exhaustive legal battles.

This is noted in the Reporters Without Borders' *Press Freedom Index*, but it has also been highlighted by the International Press Institute and the Media Rapid Response Foundation. All of these organisations are official EU partners.

Meanwhile, any story that portrays the Government in a bad light simply isn't covered. The state news agency, for instance, did not mention Greece at all in its coverage of the Press Freedom Index. While there is a network of independent outlets in the country, their stories rarely break through to the mainstream.

This has become the norm in Greece. But will the same now happen routinely within the European Parliament?

The EU appears to have no problem with what the Greek Government is doing and is happy to look the other way in exchange for Greece keeping refugees off European soil.

When contacted by Brussels-based outlet Euractiv, Maltese politician Roberta Matsola – currently President of the European Parliament – declined to comment.

Perhaps this is unsurprising as Matsola comes from the same political grouping – the European People's Party Group – as the ruling party in Greece, and its deputy leader employs Prime Minister Mitsotakis's son as an assistant.

The European Commission has now promised that its upcoming rule of law report will focus on press freedom in the EU as a whole and Greece in particular.

31 May 2022

The above information is reprinted with kind permission from *Byline Times*.
© 2023 Byline Media Holdings Ltd, Byline Times & Yes We Work Ltd

www.bylinetimes.com

We're fine as we are, press tells EU as Brussels plans media freedom law

The new proposal aims to protect media organizations from political and economic meddling – but publishers worry it could interfere in their business.

By Clothilde Goujard

Brussels has put forward a new law to protect deteriorating media freedom and pluralism across Europe – but press publishers argue it will have the opposite effect.

The European Media Freedom Act proposal aims to buffer newsrooms from political and media magnates' meddling and limit the buildup of massive media conglomerates. New rules could give media authorities a greater say over mergers, and outlets would have to disclose their owners – direct and indirect.

The Commission's plan for an EU legislation is a response to the growing threats to media freedom across the bloc. Hungary and Poland have ramped up efforts to control the media, amid wider assaults on the rule of law in both countries. The problem is much broader with journalists in Greece, Slovenia and Malta reporting under difficult conditions and pressure from their governments.

'For the first time in EU law, we are presenting safeguards to protect the editorial independence of the media,' said Commission Vice President Věra Jourová at a press conference on Friday.

The unprecedented move has press publishers – which had already tried to kill the law during consultations – up in arms.

'Media regulators can now interfere with the free press, while publishers are estranged from their own publications,' said Ilias Konteas, executive director of the European Magazine Media Association (of which POLITICO's owner Axel Springer is a member) and the European Newspaper Publishers Association.

'The press has always operated on the basis of the principle of freedom of a publisher to set up their business and work jointly with their journalists to deliver news and information to citizens in Europe and across the world.'

Unlike radio and television broadcasters, which are overseen by independent media regulators, the press in most EU countries so far has relied on self-regulation in the form of ethics codes, press and media councils, or ombudspersons.

Now, publishers' lobbies fear the law could limit their editorial control over their publications. A newly-proposed pan-European group of national media regulators is also at the centre of their worries: This body, they say, could oversee their editorial activities.

The Commission has fiercely rebutted these arguments, with top officials arguing that, contrary to publishers' criticism, the rules would instead introduce better safeguards for journalists to make independent editorial decisions.

'For some who say the EU should not regulate their media landscape in Europe, we have a message; we believe the opposite: We need to have good rules,' Jourová said.

Internal Market Commissioner Thierry Breton emphasized during a press conference that there was 'absolutely no attempt from the Commission to grab power.'

The European board would not enforce rules on the disclosure of ownership and on potential conflicts of interests that could affect editorial decisions. It would also not oversee new rules mandating that editors must be free to make individual choices, said a Commission official. Instead, if the law is passed as currently written, the rules could be used in legal disputes before courts but wouldn't be enforced by media regulators.

'What the board will do is [issue] some nonbinding opinions when it comes to [media] concentration, where there could indeed be some print media involved, but this is really totally different from saying that we are putting the press under new regulatory authority,' said a Commission official.

The independent group – which has in the past been used by audiovisual regulators to share standards – will largely advise the Commission, give opinions, coordinate on potential sanctions against foreign state-funded media sharing propaganda, and act as a forum for best practices. The body would comprise the EU's 27 national audiovisual media authorities.

Press publishers may criticize the law, but journalism and press-freedom associations, as well as broadcasters, have largely stood behind the proposal.

Nearly twenty journalism and press-freedom associations including Reporters Without Borders, Civil Liberties Union for Europe and the European Federation of Journalists said that the draft EU law should go even further to shield media from undue political and commercial interest.

Noel Curran, director general of the European Broadcasting Union, applauded the Commission's plan to 'reverse the threats that the entire media sector is facing, alongside its actions to protect the rule of law.'

The Commission's plan 'is not trying to get rid of any best practices or to undermine situations that are already able to guarantee plurality and independence of the media,' said Maria Luisa Stasi, the head of digital-markets law for ARTICLE 19, a nonprofit.

For publishers and the Commission, this is just the start of a long fight, as the plan still needs to face the careful scrutiny of the European Parliament and the EU Council, representing member countries' governments.

16 September 2022

Article was first published by POLITICO and written by POLITICO reporter Clothilde Goujard

The above information is reprinted with kind permission from POLITICO.
© 2023 POLITICO

www.politico.eu

The fine line between fake news and freedom of speech

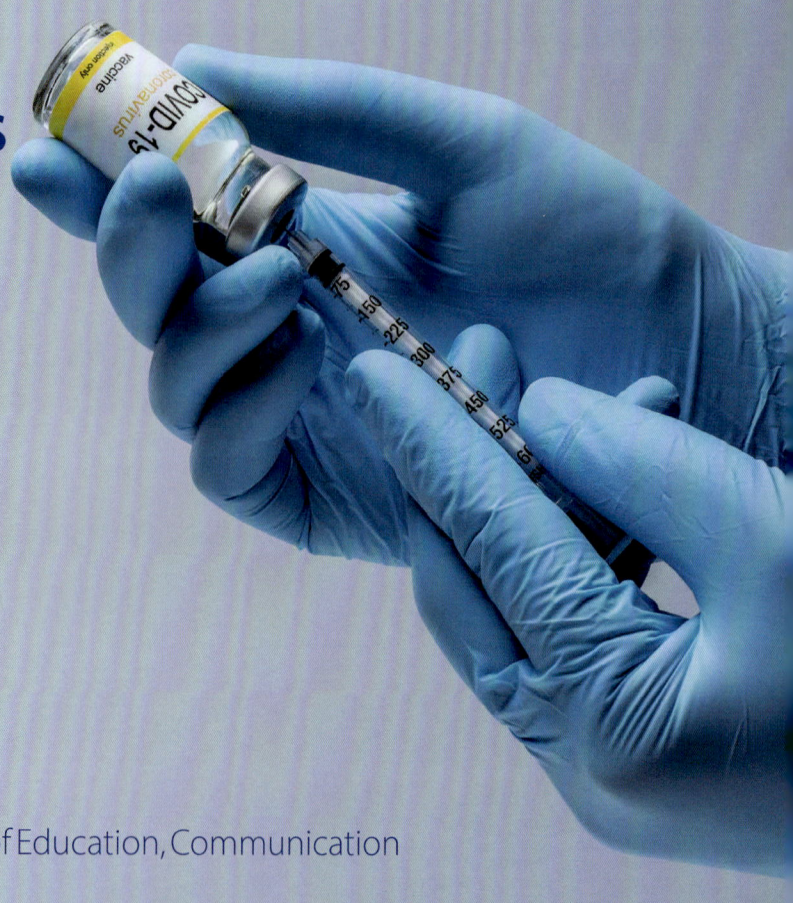

By Eva Carrillo Roas, alumna of the School of Education, Communication & Society, King's College London

With confusion and chaos comes fake news. How should we manage videos spread on social media containing false information about Covid-19 vaccines? In this post, the author looks at the video published by osteopath Dr. Carrie Madej, in which she claims that coronavirus vaccines can alter your DNA. While censorship can be efficient in stopping the spread of such videos, transparency from the government and the vaccine companies could solve the problem of mistrust.

> *'The coronavirus vaccines are designed to make us into genetically modified organisms.'* – Dr Carrie Madej

Despite fake news being around for a long time, some academics argue that we have entered a post-truth era, where media creators convince readers to believe something despite evidence against it. Since the beginning of the pandemic, we have been constantly bombarded with fake news. The lack of knowledge on the virus created a perfect environment for fake news and conspiracy theories to flourish, and confusion and mistrust increased. Therefore, it is no surprise that videos such as Madej's become viral and affect so many people.

Madej is an osteopath who uploaded a video on YouTube in June 2020, arguing that Covid-19 vaccines will alter the recipients' DNA. This video went viral, gaining over 300,000 views on YouTube, and was spread via other platforms such as Facebook, Instagram, Twitter, and WhatsApp.

Understanding fake news – What factors contribute to the rise of fake news/conspiracies?

The rise and advance of technology has undoubtedly changed the way society works and how media messages are reproduced. The decrease of traditional media networks (such as newspapers) and the simultaneous increase of social media has played a huge role in the rise of conspiracy theories.

Social media platforms such as Twitter were designed for everyone (in theory) to have a space to share and upload whatever they want (with some guidelines). And although this has led to incredible things, such as the rise of digital activism and social movements, such as #MeToo, it also created a space where misleading information can be shared by anyone at a rapid speed.

The spread of fake news via social media stems in part from the absence of fact-checking and proof-reading which other media platforms such as newspapers have to go through (although not always).

When thinking of Madej's video, we can see that, although the biological facts that she gives are not wrong, the conclusions and links she makes have not been proven to be correct; for instance, she uses the example of genetically modified food to raise the question: 'what if this can be done to humans?'.

The philosopher Lee McIntyre argues that another factor contributing to the rise of conspiracy theories is the eroding trust in science that we can see, for example, in climate change denial. However, Madej's approach is very interesting, as she is using science to prove her point, instead of completely disregarding it. Also, taking into consideration that she is a doctor, this is particularly dangerous as it gives her credibility and persuades viewers that wouldn't normally tend to fall for 'fake news' to believe her.

Is censorship the way forward?

Social media companies such as Facebook have been very active in trying to combat misleading information. Between March and October 2020, Facebook removed more than 12 million posts containing misinformation about Covid-19. But, is censorship the best way to deal with fake news and conspiracy theories?

After Madej's video went viral, social media companies such as YouTube and Facebook deleted it from their platforms (although one can still find it when searching). While censorship can be effective in stopping the spread of such misinformation, is it OK to limit freedom of speech in this way?

Freedom of speech is a huge part of our human and civil rights, but that does not mean someone should have a right to speak freely, even if they are spreading lies.

Thinking back to Madej's video, I believe that arguing that she is just sharing simple 'opinions' is dangerous. Lies and manipulation of facts have direct effects on real people. People deciding not to get the vaccine could make others ill. Thus, the line should be drawn when someone's right to freedom of speech comes hand in hand with someone getting hurt.

On the other hand, censorship does not get to the root of the problem: the mistrust in the government and Covid-19 vaccine producers. Censorship only silences the believers of conspiracy theories and gives them more reasons to believe in them as 'Why would they delete it if it wasn't true?'.

This mistrust has been built throughout the decades, as governments have done horrible things before in the name of science such as the Tuskegee experiment. Hence, it is no surprise that people mistrust governments when it wasn't so long ago that similar unimaginable things happened.

The journalist Peter Pomerantsev argues that the most effective way to combat misleading information in media is through political and scientific transparency from governments and the Covid-19 vaccine producers. Through this, he suggests, we can start to build back the trust that has been eroding for decades and combat the spread of misleading information around Covid-19, as fake news is often an outcome of ignorance.

Whether this is utopian or not is another debate, but it would seem that this approach may have started to bear fruit as media companies such as the BBC have created online sections that debunk conspiracy theories such as Madej's through scientific transparency.

18 May 2022

References on page 42.

Disclaimer: This blog and its content do not represent King's or the School of Education, Communication & Society, nor any of the academics who teach on the BA Social Sciences.

King's Social Journal

This blog is led by students from the BA Social Sciences, in King's School of Education, Communication & Society. It aims to analyse pressing issues that society faces today.

The above information is reprinted with kind permission from King's College London.
© 2023 King's College London

www.kcl.ac.uk/ecs

How Iran is suppressing protest at the World Cup by censoring players and banning journalists

Iran's players have been criticised for not joining in with dissent spreading across their homeland but the regime's crackdown on high-profile figures leaves them in a 'tricky position', experts tell *i*.

By George Simms

'I don't care if I'm sacked. Shame on you for killing people so easily. Viva Iranian women.'

These words appeared in a later-deleted Instagram post by Sardar Azmoun, one of Iran's most famous footballers. With 41 goals in 65 international appearances, the Islamic nation's World Cup hopes will depend heavily on the Bayer Leverkusen forward.

Yet there was great pressure on national team manager Carlos Queiroz not to select Azmoun for the World Cup, especially from the Iranian government. There are even calls for Iran to be removed from the tournament altogether. They now face England in the Group B opener on the afternoon of Monday 21 November.

Azmoun is aware that he is risking his chance to represent his country by publicly supporting protests sparked by the death of 22-year-old Mahsa Amini. Amini died in hospital with visible signs of having been beaten after she was arrested and detained by Iranian 'morality police' for reportedly wearing a loose hijab that revealed her hair. The Iranian government claims she died from a heart attack.

Protests have now been active in as many as 80 cities throughout Iran in the two months since Amini's death. According to Oslo-based organisation Iran Human Rights, at least 326 people have been killed in the protests, with reports of 40 people being shot dead by security services in Zahedan on one day.

There are widespread concerns within the Iranian government about potential protests by Iranian players on the global stage. There was even speculation the government would withdraw the team, or send a squad of politically pliable youngsters. But Iran are going to Qatar and Azmoun has been selected in the 26-man squad.

The Iranian beach football team, which won the Intercontinental Cup on Sunday 6 November, did not sing the national anthem before the final and the winning goal scorer imitated cutting his hair, in solidarity with the protesters.

Iran's football federation said the players would be 'dealt with according to the regulations. As per the regulations of the Islamic Republic of Iran and the Olympic Code of Ethics and the rules of FIFA, political behaviour must be avoided in sports fields.'

Iranian journalists have had their World Cup accreditation denied by the Qatari interior ministry ahead of the tournament. Iran want to limit coverage of the tournament within the country, in an attempt to limit any local reporting of potential protests by players in Qatar.

Reflecting on the possibility of losing his place in the national team, Azmoun said: '[It] is a small price to pay for even a single lock of hair from an Iranian woman.'

Once dubbed the 'Iranian Messi', Azmoun is one of many Iranian current and former footballers to express their support for the protests.

Former Bayern Munich midfielder Ali Karimi, considered one of the greatest Asian players of all time, was charged in absentia by the Iranian government in October for his support of the protests to his 14.1 million Instagram followers.

Ali Daei, another Iranian great and former Bayern Munich forward, has reportedly had his passport seized by Iranian authorities ahead of the World Cup after returning home from Istanbul recently.

On Instagram, Daei wrote: 'My homeland Iran means: my family, my father and mother, my daughters and fellow countrymen are my brothers and sisters.

'Instead of repression, violence and arresting the Iranian people, solve their problems.'

Daei and Karimi, as well as Iran's most-capped player Javad Nekounam, have all rejected invitations from FIFA to attend the upcoming World Cup. Daei said: 'I want to be with my compatriots and express sympathy with all those who have lost loved ones. Hoping for brighter days for Iran.'

Multiple other Iranian footballers and journalists have been arrested for their role in the protests. Sports photographer Yalda Moayeri, a member of the Iranian Press Photographers Association, was arrested and detained in Qarchak prison. Qarchak is known for its inhumane conditions, with no proper sewer system within the prison.

Former Iranian international Hossein Mahini, who plays for Tehran-based Saipa FC, was also arrested in October as a result of social media posts he made supporting the protests.

Other players including former Brighton and now Feyernoord winger Alireza Jahanbakhsh and Hull City forward Allahyar Sayyadmanesh have spoken out publicly. After a 1-1 draw with Senegal in Vienna during September's international break, Jahanbakhsh told Iranian state television: 'I hope from now on during home matches, our dear women can also spectate, so we can make them happy as well.'

But these statements make them a target for Iranian censorship, which Daei and Karimi have already experienced. Both Sayyadmanesh and Jahanbakhsh are based overseas but there are concerns for their family members in Iran if they continue to support the protests.

In the wake of their Iranian Super Cup win, Esteghlal players refused to cheer and the captain, Hossein Hosseini, who has been selected in the Iranian World Cup squad, dedicated the trophy to Iranian women.

Queiroz, once assistant manager of Manchester United under Sir Alex Ferguson, said on Tuesday: 'Everybody has the right to express themselves. You guys are used to kneeling in the games and some people agree, some people don't agree with that, and in Iran it's exactly the same.

'It is out of the question to think that the Iran national team is suffering any sort of issues like that. The players only have one thing in mind, which is to fight for that dream to be in the second round.'

Football and sport in general have been heavily regulated and controlled in Iran since Ayatollah Khomeini's rise to power as a result of the Iranian Revolution.

Women have been banned from attending football stadiums in Iran since 1981, with occasional access to the 78,000-seater Azadi Stadium in Tehran the only exception. The excuse given by the Iranian government is that stadiums are not considered safe for women.

Amini's death has been reminiscent of the death of Sahar Khodayari. The 29-year-old was arrested in March 2019 after attempting to watch Esteghlal at the Azadi Stadium. In order to access a game at which female fans were not allowed, she used YouTube make-up tutorials to try and pass as a man. She was unsuccessful. Khodayari was detained and held for a week in Qarchak prison.

Although there is no formal law banning women from Iran's football stadiums, she was charged with failing to respect Islamic hijab regulations, as was Amini three years later. As she left the court, Khodayari set herself on fire. She died a week later. She became known as 'the blue girl', in reference to Esteghlal's club colours. Rage at Khodayari's death was stark and powerful in Iran and across the world, but gradually it subsided and the issue was ignored once again.

Football has a history of acting as a foundation for protest across the Middle East. James Montague, author of When Friday Comes: Football Revolution in the Middle East and the Road to Qatar, told: 'When Hosni Mubarak is toppled in Egypt in 2011, who fought for that revolution? It was tens of thousands of football ultras, they were the battering ram of that revolution.

'In the aftermath of Mubarak's toppling, you would go to Tahrir Square and you would see the flags of Ah Ahly and Zamalek. The songs that I had heard sung on terraces in Cairo, they became the soundtrack of the revolution.'

Many hope that the same can be done in Iran, although there is the feeling that footballers are not doing enough. If you scroll through the comments on social media posts by top players, the overwhelming sentiment is highly critical.

'Iran's players are in a tricky position,' Montague said. 'The regime punishes dissent, even when it's out of the country. If they can't get you, they will go after your family. National team players have an elevated position so when the protest broke out it was expected they would support them.

'But, actually, the protesters viewed many of the players negatively for low-key or obtuse support. Go on Instagram and you will see, far from being hailed as heroes, they are being criticised for not doing enough. Everyone is scared of reprisals.'

Open Stadiums is a movement of Iranian women seeking to allow women free access to Iran's stadiums. There was praise across Western media when Iranian players appeared to cover their badges before a friendly against Senegal, but Open Stadiums tells *i*: 'I don't know how people assume they did this to support people. It was always like this. Nothing special happened.'

The players also received heavy criticism for meeting Iranian president Ebrahim Raisi before they left for Doha.

Open Stadiums recently published an open letter to FIFA president Gianni Infantino: 'Iranian women remain locked out of our "Beautiful Game" and we are systematically repressed when we try to enter stadiums in Iran.

'In March 2022, women who were told they could watch a FIFA World Cup 2022 qualifying match between Iran and Lebanon in Mashdad were tear-gassed and pepper-sprayed by police. When the Islamic Republic pretended to open league matches for women, it was far from the equality FIFA's own statutes require.

'To begin with, very few women could buy tickets, then in a humiliating way got physically harassed by Iran's morality police before they could even enter Azadi stadium, which to this day is the only stadium in the country where women have been allowed to watch men's matches at all.'

Open Stadiums expressed concerns that Iranian agents will travel to Qatar to monitor and control Iranian fans, particularly women, with potential consequences upon their return.

Open Stadiums has also called for Iran to be banned from the tournament, claiming that the nation's 'gender apartheid' is in convention of FIFA's statutes.

Open Stadiums is not alone in these demands. The Ukrainian federation urged FIFA to remove Iran from the World Cup, citing human rights violations and supplying the Russian military with weapons.

The Ukrainian FA has not asked for Iran to be replaced by Ukraine, although this was mentioned in an appeal by Shakhtar Donetsk.

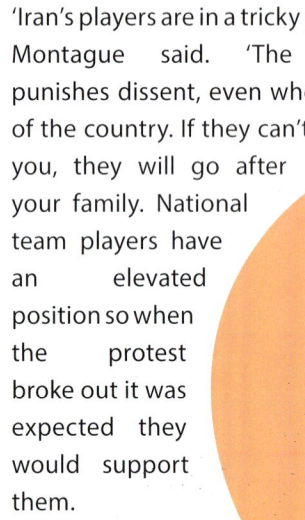

'Ukraine has a good case,' Montague said. 'Russia was essentially suspended from football because it invaded Ukraine and Iran is supplying loitering munitions and drones targeting civilian infrastructure. This is a war crime, but it is very late in the day.'

Ashok Swain, Unesco chair of Uppsala University in Sweden and professor within its Department of Peace and Conflict Research, was sceptical of calls to ban Iran. 'Banning sports does not help the cause. It has not in the past, and it will not do now,' Swain said.

He also raised questions about foreign involvement, saying: 'International support for a protest in a closed country like Iran is a double-edged sword.

'The support from fans across the world will be a morale booster for the protesting masses in Iran, and at the same it will also help the regime to carry its propaganda that the protest is a foreign conspiracy.'

The support of figures like Azmoun is highly significant within Iran, although multiple international stars, including the Chelsea and England defender Reece James, have publicly declared their support for protests.

'The support of the Iranian team is more powerful than other footballers doing it,' Swain adds.

It is highly unlikely that FIFA will take any action against the Iranian team ahead of the finals. Its regulations are deliberately vague, stating that FIFA 'remains neutral in matters of politics and religion' and that 'exceptions may be made with regard to matters affected by FIFA's statutory objectives'.

Women have recently been allowed into Azadi Stadium for internationals, but Open Stadiums wrote that 'many believe the Azadi stadium has been opened for a short-term PR stunt to enhance the Iranian Football Association's image before FIFA's showcase World Cup'.

The eyes of the world will remain on Iran throughout the World Cup. It is vital that this scrutiny and pressure continues well beyond their exit from the competition.

8 November 2022

Research

In pairs, research sporting events that have been censored, such as the Olympics and the World Cup. Can you find any examples of what was censored?

The above information is reprinted with kind permission from *i News*.
© 2023 Associated Newspapers Limited

www.inews.co.uk

Nobel Prize underscores risks to journalists and democracy

Press freedom is under assault around the world and journalists are in increased danger. The Nobel Peace Prize highlights threats to the Fourth Estate.

By Nelson Graves

By awarding the Nobel Peace Prize to two journalists who have risked their lives by speaking truth to power, the Nobel Committee has reminded us of the mortal dangers that many reporters face in doing their job and the crucial role journalists play in defending democracy.

The award, given to journalists for only the third time in the 120-year history of the prize, comes amid a steady deterioration in press freedom around the world and increased risks for journalists.

Maria Ressa of the Philippines and Dmitry Muratov of Russia won the annual prize for their efforts to safeguard the freedom of expression.

'They are representatives of all journalists who stand up for this ideal in a world in which democracy and freedom of the press face increasingly adverse conditions,' the Nobel Committee said in awarding the prize last week.

Nobel Prize highlights how journalists run increased risks.

The Philippines has long been one of the most dangerous places in the world for journalists to work. Since 1992, 87 journalists have been killed in that country, according to the Committee to Protect Journalists (CPJ).

Two years ago, News Decoder wrote about efforts by Ressa and her compatriot Fernando Garcia Sepe Jr. to expose corruption and abusive practices in the Southeast Asian nation.

Muratov founded the independent Russian newspaper Novaya Gazeta in 1993 and since then six of the newspaper's journalists have been killed.

The number of journalists murdered in retaliation for their work more than doubled in 2020, as criminal gangs and militant groups targeted reporters working in violent but democratic nations, according to the CPJ.

The CPJ said the number of journalists jailed globally because of their work hit a new high in 2020 as governments cracked down on coverage of COVID-19 or tried to suppress reporting on political unrest.

Protecting journalists to protect democracy

Aralynn McMane, founder of the Global Youth & Media Prize and a member of the board of News Decoder's governing non-profit, has compiled a useful list of resources detailing threats to journalists around the world (see www.globalyouthandnewsmediaprize.net/resource-threats-to-journalists).

She cites a report by Reporters Without Borders (RSF) that showed that journalism is completely or partly blocked in 73% of the 180 countries ranked by the NGO, which noted a dramatic deterioration in people's access to information and an increase in obstacles to news coverage. 'Journalism is the best vaccine against disinformation,' RSF secretary-general Christophe Deloire said.

She also cites Ressa's interview of human rights lawyer Amal Clooney.

On World Press Freedom day earlier this year, News Decoder broadcast a webinar, in association with the United Nations Educational, Scientific and Cultural Organization (UNESCO), on the topic of protecting journalists to protect democracy.

The session featured CPJ Deputy Executive Director Robert Mahoney, Indiana University Professor Elaine Monaghan and eight students from News Decoder partner schools in Belgium, Denmark, South Korea and the United States.

14 October 2021

Three questions to consider...

1. What does the expression 'to speak truth to power' mean?
2. What do you think that in some countries, COVID-19 led to curbs on press freedom?
3. How free is the press in your country?

The above information is reprinted with kind permission from News Decoder.
© News Decoder 2023

www.news-decoder.com

2021: a grim year for journalists and free speech in an increasingly turbulent and authoritarian world

An article from The Conversation.

By Dina Matar, Professor, Political Communication and Arab Media, SOAS, University of London

Hundreds of journalists killed or arrested, rising numbers of female media workers targeted, floods of misinformation and hate speech and ineffectual or hostile governments unable or unwilling to protect the public's right to know. The 2021 press freedom index released recently by Reporters Without Borders (RSF) makes for grim reading.

The report reveals that 488 journalists were detained in 2021 – an increase of 20% compared to the previous year – while a total of 46 were killed and 65 held hostage. Of those detained, 60 were women (33% higher than 2020). As you might expect, it tends to be autocratic regimes with dismal records for freedom of speech and human rights which crop up once again as the worst offenders.

The latest report notes an upturn in repression against journalists in Belarus – where opposition politicians and commentators have been targeted in the government crackdown since the August 2020 election – as well in Myanmar, where the military coup of February has been followed by a crackdown on free expression. In China, where the Communist party continues to tighten its grip, and Hong Kong, where the Beijing-backed regime is using the draconian national security law to punish dissidents, it gets ever more perilous to oppose the increasingly authoritarian regime of Xi Jinping.

These findings linking authoritarian governments to human rights abuses are not surprising given the tendency of such governments to use local and global crises – such as COVID at present – to clamp down on press freedom under the guise of national interest and security.

Bullying, hate speech and censorship

Journalists are facing increasing threats for doing their jobs – whether that is physical intimidation, hate speech directed against them or online trolling. Some European countries have used the law to prevent the dissemination of information that political actors see as threatening their hold on power and legitimacy. We've seen that in Spain, for example, where parties on both sides of politics have gone out of their way to stigmatise the media and hamper the free flow of information, even banning some journalists from press conferences.

Such practices, which include interference in the daily work of media outlets, as well as implicit and explicit threats to journalists doing their job, are well documented in the 2021 report by the One Free Press Coalition which mapped such acts in a variety of European countries since 2014. Elsewhere, including in Iran, Syria, Mexico, Sudan and Guatemala, intimidation is creating a climate of fear among media professionals. This prevents the free circulation of information, opinions and ideas. It also allows for the wider circulation of fake news and misinformation.

What is of concern is the risk that such acts of intimidation against journalists and the media can become normalised – even in western democracies.

In response to the alarming rise in attacks against journalists worldwide, the United Nations designated November 2nd each year as the International Day to End Impunity for Crimes Against Journalists. The designation is symbolic – but a serious engagement with ending impunity for crimes against journalists can form the basis for a legal framework that can guarantee freedom of expression and access to information and ensure journalists carry out their jobs.

Profession under threat

Throughout history, people practising journalism have faced intimidation and attacks for a variety of reasons, whether it is governments worried about exposure or partisan and private interests worried about their profits. But what the increasing number of attacks suggests is that journalism is becoming more and more a contested domain and space for struggle over information, ideology and politics.

These attacks violate human rights: both of journalists and the societies they serve which are being deprived of their right to information – something that should be at the heart of all free public debate and the democratic process. They underscore the need for adequate legal protection for journalists that goes beyond rights to communicate and free speech recognised in particularly in Article 19 of the Universal Declaration of Human Rights.

Article 19 recognises everyone's right to freedom of opinion and expression and provides the basis for the function of journalism, conducted by individuals, to be protected – independently of broader institutional press or media rights. In international law, freedom to express opinions and ideas is considered essential at both an individual level, insofar as it contributes to the full development of a person, and also as a foundation stone of democratic society.

International human rights law requires states to respect and protect the lives of all within their jurisdiction from attacks and threats of attacks and to provide an effective remedy where this has not been the case. But so far there is no international framework dedicated to the protection of journalists from physical attack or ending impunity for crimes against journalists. If journalists are deliberately targeted and threatened while those who attack them go unpunished, the media cannot be free and democracy will continue to be threatened.

23 December 2021

THE CONVERSATION

The above information is reprinted with kind permission from The Conversation.
© 2010-2023, The Conversation Trust (UK) Limited

www.theconversation.com

Five questions for every newsroom to ask themselves on World Press Freedom Day

World Press Freedom Day is a reminder of why democracy and a free press matter. But conversations about safety, sustainability and sourcing need to be an all-year priority.

By Catherine Edwards

Journalists covering conflicts, as well as those working in authoritarian or hostile environments, are rightly at the front of our minds on World Press Freedom Day, a day of support for media vulnerable to press freedom attacks, and a day to remember journalists who have lost their lives because of their work.

Press freedom cannot be taken for granted, and the press can be silenced in new and different ways. That is demonstrated by this year's theme of the 'digital siege' or the rise of digital authoritarianism. Global Voices describes this as 'how digital communications technologies are being used to advance authoritarian governance around the world.' The team picked out a selection of stories which have not received the attention they warrant. Many of these cases come from countries where attacks on the press have long been part of the modus operandi of illiberal regimes, but wherever you are based, press freedom is not something that can be taken for granted.

A good example of that comes from an editorial in the *Toronto Star,* showing how even in Canada, intimidation and harassment of journalists is rife - while the Reporters Without Borders Press Freedom Index only described the press freedom situation as 'good' in 26 of 180 countries.

Statements from the International Press Institute and European Federation of Journalists have equally highlighted the need for democracies to stand up for press freedom at home.

And while journalists cannot always influence decisions made by politicians or platforms that transform the environment we work in, every newsroom can play a part in securing the future of the industry. Here are five questions every newsroom should be considering this World Press Freedom Day.

How resilient are our revenue streams?

Media viability is a press freedom issue. Without money, there is no journalism.

Free Press Unlimited summarises some of the major threats to viable independent media, including media capture (direct or indirect control of media by the state, for example through ownership or advertising) and financial pressure. The covid-19 pandemic has only intensified the economic threat to the news industry, in particular by accelerating the decline of newspaper revenue, as new research by *Economist Impact* shows.

As a result, newsrooms should regularly audit where their money comes from, keeping abreast of changes and policies which could impact that income.

Developing multiple revenue sources is critical. Newsrooms around the world have secured their independence through carving out membership models and consultancy work within their business.

Journalists walking out of compromised newsrooms and rebooting with a new venture supported directly by readers has become an increasingly common occurrence - see *Telex* in Hungary and *Kyiv Independent* in Ukraine. The founders of both organisations spoke at the International Journalism Festival about how their survival was made possible through reader donations and subscriptions.

Outside repressive regimes, reader funding brings closer connections to community while ensuring independence. To name just two very different examples of outlets where this applies, both *Black Ballad*, the UK news platform for young Black women, and the Croatian investigative outlet *Telegram* have experimented successfully with reader revenue.

Do we protect our journalists from harassment?

Abuse is not part of the job description for journalists, but with increasing polarisation and journalists often needing to be active on social media to find stories and communicate with their communities, it is something many are exposed to.

For journalists to be able to work safely and effectively - and for newsrooms to retain talented staff - their employers must support them.

The International Press Institute and International Women's Media Foundation both offer online courses in building a strategy to prevent abuse and protect staff if it happens, while the Rory Peck Trust and Freelance Journalism Assembly provide safety resources for freelancers.

Are we supporting our colleagues working in dangerous situations?

To report on global news, most newsrooms rely on the bravery and professionalism of colleagues on the ground in difficult environments.

In response to the crisis in Ukraine, the international media community mobilised quickly to provide financial and material support, but some of those on the ground pointed out that despite the solidarity, many outlets continue to fail to offer the support and credit these journalists need.

Journalists who are sent on assignment to hostile environments should be given adequate training and preparation, and support on their return. And when working with local journalists and producers, there are practical steps to take to ensure their safety, such as paying them promptly and fairly, not requiring them to be in physically dangerous situations unnecessarily, and giving them credit for their work.

The Committee to Protect Journalists has a wealth of resources in its Security Guide.

Who are we speaking to?

The latest edition of the Press Freedom Index from Reporters Without Borders highlights how growing polarisation provides a fertile ground for the spread of disinformation and tension, which in the worst cases can fuel conflicts. So, is your newsroom doing enough to reach across divides and represent marginalised groups?

Many organisations are doing excellent work in this area, from Deutsche Welle's Flipping the Script project putting voters at the centre of election coverage, to the People's Newsroom at the Bureau Local. By reaching out to groups traditionally under-represented in the news - and working with them ethically and responsibly - your journalism can help readers better understand people and issues they do not come into contact with in everyday life.

Journalists should also consider whether they are doing enough to reach young people, typically turned off by mainstream reporting but with a strong interest in the news, and to reach groups that have low levels of engagement with politics. This includes keeping up with evolving formats and news behaviours, and reviewing things like headlines and picture choices to ensure they accurately represent your reporting even to those who only skim their news feed.

Are we doing enough to build trust?

This is perhaps the most crucial question to ask. If audiences do not trust you, they certainly will not support you. The good news is that anybody and everybody in the newsroom can be part of the solution.

Building trust is an ongoing process, involving everything from transparency around your data collection practices and advertising, to your relationships with community members, and the way you respond to corrections and criticism.

Helpful resources are available from the Trust Project which shares eight key indicators and the Trusting News Project which offers case studies and tips on building trust, while the Reuters Institute for the Study of Journalism's Trust in News project has carried out research into why people do not trust the news, so that you can use this to inform your own trust strategy.

World Press Freedom Day is a chance to communicate the necessity of free media, but newsrooms have a responsibility to demonstrate their value by building trust year-round. We would love to hear how your newsroom is thinking about and responding to these challenges.

3 May 2022

Catherine Edwards is acting editor of Journalism.co.uk, and also works with the International Press Institute and Free Press for Eastern Europe on projects supporting newsrooms across Central and Eastern Europe.

The above information is reprinted with kind permission from journalism.co.uk
© 2023 Mousetrap Media Ltd

www.journalism.co.uk

Freedom of Expression

Chapter 3

Freedom of expression is key to countering disinformation

Disinformation is by no means a new concern, yet a recent report of the UN Secretary-General aims to address the phenomenon of disinformation in the context of new and rapidly evolving communications landscapes, due to innovative technologies, which have enabled the dissemination of unparalleled volumes of content at unprecedented speeds.

'Disinformation comes in different forms, this includes targeted operations by states, state officials, conspiracy fed theories about health policies and vaccines, smear campaigns to undermine specific groups and persons and many others,' said Assistant Secretary General for Human Rights, Ilze Brands-Kehris, while presenting the Secretary-General's report to the General Assembly.

The report states that navigating the modern media landscapes and ensuring it advances, rather than undermines, human rights, international peace and security is a key challenge of the digital age.

A major challenge posed by disinformation is its lack of definition said Agustina Del Campo, Director of the Center for Studies on Freedom of Expression and Access to Information (CELE) and Vice-President of the Global Network Initiative (GNI).

'[It is] a broad term used to describe complex phenomena, for which there is no universally agreed definition,' she said.

In a high-level panel discussion held at the Human Rights Council earlier this year, participants stressed that the spread of disinformation can have a negative impact on societies, undermining a broad range of human rights. They noted that when disinformation threatens human rights, States have a duty to take appropriate steps to address these harmful impacts.

However, 'disinformation should not become a pretext to intimidate and harass critical voices, denigrate opponents, justify censorship, or obstruct the legitimate activities of human rights defenders and the media to access and disseminate information,' said Brands-Kehris. 'Responses to disinformation should be grounded in respect for freedom of expression,' she added while presenting the report to the General Assembly.

One way in which States can help reduce the risks associated with disinformation is by creating the conditions for human rights, pluralism and tolerance to flourish, the report states. The Special Rapporteur on freedom of opinion and expression, Irene Khan stressed that 'if independent public interest media cannot survive – let alone thrive – disinformation will flourish, journalists will be further imperilled and societies' right to information will be undermined.'

The report describes media and digital literacy initiatives to enhance the capacities of all stakeholders to identify, dispel and debunk false and misleading information as one tool to address disinformation.

States are central players in efforts to address the evolving challenges and impact posed by disinformation, yet other actors also have a critical role to play. Public officials have heightened responsibilities to avoid disseminating disinformation, companies should expand transparency around their policies and responses to disinformation and expand research access to data to support more evidence-based responses and regulations, Brands-Kehris stressed.

'Governments should work to build trust including through strengthening media space and information literacy, empowering individuals to identify, critically analyze and counter disinformation in an enabling environment to make their voices heard in debates and decision-making,' Brands-Kehris said.

3 November 2022

The above information is reprinted with kind permission from United Nations Human Rights Office of the High Commissioner.

© OHCHR 1996-2023

www.ohchr.org

Article 10: Freedom of expression

Article 10 protects your right to hold your own opinions

Article 10 protects your right to hold your own opinions and to express them freely without government interference.

This includes the right to express your views aloud (for example through public protest and demonstrations) or through:

- published articles, books or leaflets
- television or radio broadcasting
- works of art
- the internet and social media

The law also protects your freedom to receive information from other people by, for example, being part of an audience or reading a magazine.

Are there any restrictions to this right?

Although you have freedom of expression, you also have a duty to behave responsibly and to respect other people's rights.

Public authorities may restrict this right if they can show that their action is lawful, necessary and proportionate in order to:

- protect national security, territorial integrity (the borders of the state) or public safety
- prevent disorder or crime
- protect health or morals
- protect the rights and reputations of other people
- prevent the disclosure of information received in confidence
- maintain the authority and impartiality of judges

An authority may be allowed to restrict your freedom of expression if, for example, you express views that encourage racial or religious hatred.

However, the relevant public authority must show that the restriction is 'proportionate', in other words that it is appropriate and no more than necessary to address the issue concerned.

Using this right – example

This right is particularly important for journalists and other people working in the media.

They must be free to criticise the government and our public institutions without fear of prosecution – this is a vital feature of a democratic society.

But that doesn't prevent the state from imposing restrictions on the media in order to protect other human rights, such as a person's right to respect for their private life.

Example case - *Observer* and *The Guardian* v United Kingdom [1991]

The Guardian and *The Observer* newspapers published excerpts from Peter Wright's book *Spycatcher*, which included allegations that MI5 had acted unlawfully.

The government obtained a court order preventing the newspapers from printing further material until proceedings relating to a breach of confidence had finished.

But when the book was published, *The Guardian* complained that the continuation of the court order infringed the right to freedom of expression.

The European Court of Human Rights said that the court order was lawful because it was in the interests of national security.

However, it also said that that wasn't enough reason to continue the newspaper publication ban once the book had been published, because the information was no longer confidential anyway.

This case summary is taken from 'Human rights, human lives: a guide to the Human Rights Act for public authorities'.

Last updated: 3 June 2021

What the law says

This text is taken directly from the Human Rights Act.

Article 10 of the Human Rights Act: Freedom of expression

1. Everyone has the right to freedom of expression. This right shall include freedom to hold opinions and to receive and impart information and ideas without interference by public authority and regardless of frontiers. This Article shall not prevent States from requiring the licensing of broadcasting, television or cinema enterprises.

2. The exercise of these freedoms, since it carries with it duties and responsibilities, may be subject to such formalities, conditions, restrictions or penalties as are prescribed by law and are necessary in a democratic society, in the interests of national security, territorial disorder or crime, for the protection of health or morals, for the protection of the reputation or rights of others, for preventing the disclosure of information received in confidence, or for maintaining the authority and impartiality of the judiciary.

The above information is reprinted with kind permission from Equality and Human Rights Commission.
© 2023 Equality and Human Rights Commission

www.equalityhumanrights.org

Freedom of speech? Not these days, if you're an artist in Britain

Following two chilling actions against artworks, the right is revealing a disturbing autocratic tendency.

By Rhiannon Lucy Cosslett

One of the many things that studying history taught me, and which I have never forgotten, is how to recognise the typical characteristics of fascism. It's become a sort of mental list to which I turn from time to time when considering our current political situation. 'Powerful and continuing nationalism' (tick); 'disregard for human rights' (what was that about offshore asylum camps?); 'rampant cronyism and corruption' (you bet).

Then, of course, there's 'disrespect for intellectuals and the arts' – something that had been festering long before the Brexit vote but became even more explicit then, with ministers' contempt for 'experts'.

It seems people have had enough of artists too, if two recent incidents are anything to go by. First, we had a police raid on Antepavilion, an east London arts complex. Footage emerged of black- and navy-clad helmeted police (some of the helmets had union flags on them, a nice touch) forcing entry to the building. The venue's best known exhibit is a rooftop bamboo and cable structure called All Along the Watchtower. The structure resembles those that were used during Extinction Rebellion (XR) protests last year when the environmental campaigners blockaded the printing presses of Murdoch papers (XR were planning further protests at the time, which likely explains the motives behind the raid).

However, the artist Damien Meade says this sculpture was part of an architectural competition and was not affiliated to XR. Moreover, it took six weeks to install, so could not play any role in a protest at short notice. Five people were arrested and then released without charge.

The second incident involved a group of Conservative councillors in Southend-on-Sea, who succeeded in removing the installation How to Make a Bomb: An English Garden by the artist Gabriella Hirst.

The work, situated in Shoeburyness in Essex, centres on a nearly extinct species of rose that was created and registered under the name Rosa floribunda Atom Bomb in 1953. It took the form of a rose garden with benches adorned with plaques detailing Britain's nuclear history, and containing statements such as: 'The garden is a reminder that the red rose of England is entangled with an Imperial past of 'gardening the world', which has continued into a dangerously over-armed present'.

The councillors objected to one such plaque, which highlighted the devastating impact of British nuclear tests on Indigenous lands in Australia in the 1950s and 60s. They asked for it to be removed or reworded, with one councillor calling it 'a direct far left wing attack on our History, our People, and our Democratically Elected Government' (authoritarians just love an unnecessary capitalisation), and threatened to contact the media. As a result of the councillors' campaign, the artwork has been taken down, with Metal, the organisation that co-commissioned the work (alongside artists' charity the Old Waterworks), saying it did so to protect its staff.

Both of these incidents are chilling. For all their proclamations about protecting freedom of speech, in their interactions with artists the Conservatives are revealing a disturbing autocratic tendency. The same is true of the government's attitude towards academics, as the latest higher education (freedom of speech) bill demonstrates. The Tories have been convincing large parts of the electorate that they are the true custodians of British history, and that the 'woke brigade' will tear down every statue in the land if it has its way. It's blatant hypocrisy.

In 2018 there was a furore over the temporary removal of John William Waterhouse's Hylas and the Nymphs – which depicts nude girls – as part of the artist Sonia Boyce's residency at the Manchester Art Gallery. Amid the row, barely anyone seemed to care that the takedown took place during a performance art piece.

Instead, the action was framed in the media as censorship and taken entirely in bad faith, by rightwing and liberal commentators alike. The latter seemed to give scarcely any thought to the damage wrought by going along with an argument set by the cynical and the reactionary.

The original intent behind the act of removal, a conversation about what and who hangs in a gallery and why, was completely lost. By reframing Boyce's attempts at discussion and contextualisation as censorship, the right was winning an early battle in the culture war. Yet who is really attacking artists and cultural institutions?

There's a longstanding joke, as popularised by *The Young Ones*, that leftwing people go around calling other people fascists all the time. Perhaps there are times when we are overzealous, but sometimes it feels as though, while everyone was busy guarding the statue of Winston Churchill, a separate agenda was cranking into gear about other works of art. As Meade wrote in the aftermath of the police raid, historical statues are protected by laws that give offenders up to 10 years in prison, but if the artwork is deemed subversive, 'the full muscle of the state comes knocking'.

Call me a doomsayer if you want, but I'll keep ticking off that list.

20 July 2021

The above information is reprinted with kind permission from *The Guardian*.
© 2023 Guardian News and Media Limited

www.theguardian.com

Salman Rushdie's battle for free speech has been lost, friends say

Supporters claim censorship is now so rife that the author would struggle to publish *The Satanic Verses* today.

By Patrick Sawer, Senior News Reporter

Sir Salman Rushdie's fight for freedom of expression has been 'lost', according to his friends and supporters, with censorship now so rife that the author would struggle to publish *The Satanic Verses* today.

Rushdie's determination to keep voicing his vision free of dogmatic strictures has been severely undermined by extremist religious leaders and society's willingness to accommodate them, they say.

Their comments came after Rushdie continued to receive emergency medical treatment in hospital after being stabbed up to 15 times at a literary festival in western New York State.

Frances D'Souza, his close friend, said: 'No one anywhere should ever, ever, be threatened with death for writing a novel, yet we seem to be living in a world, despite Salman's fight, where that could be a possibility.

'There are other instances around the world - especially say, in India - where people are threatened with death because they have written something,' she said on the Today programme.

'It is a very sad end to this that we have it almost as a norm that if you offend a certain sector of a religious minority or majority then your life is in danger. That is medieval.'

Rushdie has laboured under the threat of death since a fatwa was imposed on him by the Iranian regime 33 years ago following the publication of *The Satanic Verses* in 1988.

Baroness D'Souza added: 'Even though Rushdie made a strong stance for free speech I'm not sure it has worked, because I think that anyone who would wish to publish something even vaguely anti-Islamic would not be touched by any publisher for a start, but would also subject him or herself to enormous danger.

'It [the fatwa against Rushdie] was the beginning of something really evil in our society and censorship is very much on the agenda these days.'

Another friend of his said the book that prompted the fatwa would be seen as too controversial to be released today.

Lisa Appignanesi, the British-Canadian writer and former president of the writers' organisation English PEN, said: '*Satanic Verses* certainly wouldn't be [published]. There are a lot of fanatical religions in the world at the moment and no one knows where the greatest terror will come from next.'

Key Fact
- Author Sir Salman Rushdie had a 'fatwa' imposed on him by the Iranian regime following the publication of his book ***The Satanic Verses*** in 1988.

Critics 'lost the battle, but won the war'

Ms Appignanesi said it was ironic that the book had been seized on by hardline Islamists as it was not a critique of Islam, but of the Britain of the time.

'*Satanic Verses* is a satire of Thatcher's Britain, not of Islam,' she told Radio 4's *Today Programme*. 'And a lot of things he describes are very much still with us, such as the tragedy of migrants and the extraordinary racism that still exists.'

Both women praised Rushdie's bravery in confronting the threat to freedom of expression and supporting other writers who faced similar attacks.

Kenan Malik, the author of *From Fatwa to Jihad: How the World Changed From the Satanic Verses to Charlie Hebdo*, said: 'The boundaries of free speech, the boundaries of restrictions on offence, on blasphemy, have got much tighter, over the past 30 to 35 years partly as a response to the Rushdie affair.

'In some ways the critics of Rushdie lost the battle, but they won the war. They lost the battle because the novel *Satanic Verses* continues to be published, but they won the war in the sense that the argument at the heart of that claim, that it is wrong to give offence to certain people, certain groups and religions and so on, has become much more mainstream.

'You could say that many societies have internalised a fatwa and introduced a form of self censorship in the way we were talking about each other.'

13 August 2022

The above information is reprinted with kind permission from *The Telegraph*.
© Telegraph Media Group Limited 2022

www.telegraph.co.uk

Without blasphemy the West would have no free speech

Salman Rushdie is the latest in a long line of heretical heroes.

By Mick Hume, Columnist

The attempt by an apparent supporter of the Islamic regime of Iran to murder British author Salman Rushdie for the crime of 'blasphemy' might seem to reveal an East-West divide. But in truth battles over blasphemy have always been a central part of the struggle for free speech within the West itself.

Without those heretical heroes of history who were prepared to question prevailing orthodoxies and face down accusations of blaspheming, there would be no freedom of speech in Western societies.

Today we still have to defend the liberty to blaspheme – in modern parlance, we might call it the right to be offensive – not only against Islam and all religions, but also against the new secular restrictions on freedom of thought and speech.

'Blasphemy' has its origins in the Ancient Greek words for 'injure' and 'speech'. The Greek 'blasphemia' described any impious speech or slander. Though, historically, blasphemy laws have been used in the West to punish attacks on or insults to the official Christian religion, blasphemy laws have also often been wielded in the West against critics of the established political and social order, since church and state were always closely linked.

In this, allegations of blasphemy have long been closely aligned with charges of heresy – the expression of ideas that go against the prevailing fundamental beliefs of a society, religious or otherwise.

The origins of heresy are revealing. An early Christian leader defined his own views as 'orthodox', from the Greek for 'right belief'. The views of his opponents he branded as heresy, from the Greek for 'choice of belief'.

So, the thing that has always got you labelled a heretic is the desire to choose what you believe and dissent from the authoritative dogma of the day. Otherwise known as the demand for freedom of thought and speech.

Free speech was never a gift handed down by the gods. It has had to be fought for time and again against church and state authorities which brand their critics as blasphemers and heretics. Rushdie is the latest in a long line of free-speech heroes who have suffered for their 'blasphemous' beliefs in the West.

It was in Ancient Athens that the idea of free speech made its first appearance in human history. Even there, however, the ruling citizens' assembly voted to put the philosopher Socrates to death because he did not 'believe in the gods that the city believes in' and was 'corrupting the youth' with his heretical ideas.

It would be some 2,000 years later before the demand for free speech in its modern form took off, in the context of the Reformation and the Enlightenment. Today, when religion is often cast as the villain in the struggle for freedom, it is worth remembering that this struggle began as a demand for religious freedom.

In the first wave of the free-speech wars in England and across Europe, those demanding more freedom were religious heretics. Advocates of the new Protestant religions wanted to break from the control of the Church of Rome, to preach and worship in their own way, and to have a Bible printed in their own language. As punishment for such heresy, both the book and the printer could be burned. William Tyndale, who famously printed a banned English version of the Bible, was accused of 'blasphemous heresy', executed by strangulation and then burned at the stake in 1536.

That was barely the beginning of the battles over blasphemy and free speech in Europe. In 1600, the Italian friar-philosopher-astrologer Giordano Bruno was burnt at the stake in Rome's Campo de Fiori, his tongue tied down to suppress his 'wicked words'. Bruno had been condemned by the pope and the Roman Inquisition for denying the truth of core Catholic doctrines such as the virgin birth, and refusing to renounce his 'heretical' beliefs. His books were banned.

Then, in 1633, the Roman Inquisition infamously struck again, judging the Renaissance scientist and philosopher Galileo Galilei to be 'vehemently suspect of heresy' for holding the Copernican view that God's Earth was not the centre of the universe. Galileo was forced to recant and was sentenced to lifelong house arrest, his blasphemous offending book was also removed from public view.

Nor did the Roman Catholic Church have a monopoly on persecuting free-thinking heretics. In 1656, the Jewish elders of Amsterdam expelled the great Enlightenment thinker Spinoza from the synagogue and community for committing 'abominable heresies' against their orthodoxies. Spinoza refused to be silenced, famously capturing the essence of the issue with his statement that, 'In a free state, every man may think what he likes and say what he thinks'.

Back in English politics, the Crown and its supporters wielded their laws against blasphemy and heresy during the revolutionary upheavals of the mid-17th century, while free-thinking rebels such as Leveller John Lilburne demanded an end to such Crown control of the printing press as 'expressly opposed and dangerous to the liberties of the people'.

The last person to be hanged for blasphemy in Britain was Thomas Aikenhead, a 20-year-old Scotsman, executed in Edinburgh in 1697. Young Aikenhead's ridiculing of Jesus Christ's miracles might sound to us like the equivalent of a modern student's drunken outburst. But the Scottish authorities insisted on hanging him as an example to others not to speak out of order.

Even after heretics were spared the gallows, the use of blasphemy laws against critics of the system continued. John Wilkes, a heroic fighter for press freedom and democracy as well as a rogue and pornographer, was imprisoned by parliament in the 1760s for both 'seditious libel' and 'blasphemous libel'. Thousands of Londoners rioted for 'Wilkes and liberty!' and almost lynched the then prime minister, Lord North.

Later British protests for democratic reform and giving ordinary people the vote were met with repression, culminating in the Peterloo Massacre of 1819. In response, the government of Lord Liverpool imposed new laws to suppress the protests and the radical free press, including increasing the penalty for publishing 'blasphemous or seditious libels' against the authorities to 14 years transportation – that is, banishment to a penal colony.

Even as democratic reforms and new freedoms were being won in the Victorian age, the attempts to outlaw heretical ideas continued. In 1859, the philosopher JS Mill published his classic case for free speech, *On Liberty*. In that same year, Charles Darwin finally published his magnum opus outlining the theory of evolution, *On the Origin of Species*. It was quickly banned as blasphemous from the library of Trinity College, Cambridge, the university where Darwin had studied.

All of that might seem a long time ago. The last successful prosecution for blasphemy in Britain was a private case, brought by the moral crusader Mary Whitehouse against *Gay News* in 1977, over a poem in which a Roman centurion described having post-crucifixion sex with a gay Jesus. The offences of blasphemy and blasphemous libel were finally abolished by the New Labour government in 2008.

Yet today the old offences of blasphemy and heresy have simply been redefined and updated. Hate-speech laws – now far more prevalent in the West than blasphemy laws – have effectively made thoughtcrimes of speech that can be branded racist, homophobic, transphobic or Islamophobic, among other '-phobias'.

Meanwhile, our culture of conformism and the fear of giving offence means that a heretical book, such as *The Satanic Verses*, would not be touched by many major publishers today.

In the *Old Testament* book of *Leviticus*, God tells Moses that 'Whoever blasphemes the name of the Lord should surely be put to death. All the congregation shall stone him.' In the modern woke equivalent, whoever blasphemes against, say, trans ideology should surely be cancelled, and all the Twitterati shall condemn him – or, more often, her.

Standing up for the freedom to question everything and say the apparently unsayable is as vital today as ever before. In the April 1989 edition of *Living Marxism* magazine (deceased), I wrote an editorial in response to outrage over *The Satanic Verses* entitled 'Defend the right to be offensive'. It suggested that 'blasphemy is part of the business... of all those who want to rid society of backward conventions and ideas', and that 'upholding the right to be offensive means rejecting any and all censorship'. Much has changed in the past 30-odd years, but some principles surely remain.

At a time when we face a new divide over freedom of expression in British and Western society, it is time for blasphemers of the world to unite in defence of heretical free speech.

16 August 2022

Key Facts

- 'Blasphemy' has its origins in the Ancient Greek words for 'injure' and 'speech'. The Greek 'blasphemia' described any impious speech or slander.

- Allegations of blasphemy have long been closely aligned with charges of heresy. The origins of heresy are revealing. An early Christian leader defined his own views as 'orthodox', from the Greek for 'right belief'. The views of his opponents he branded as heresy, from the Greek for 'choice of belief'.

- William Tyndale, who famously printed a banned English version of the Bible, was accused of 'blasphemous heresy', executed by strangulation and then burned at the stake in 1536.

- The last person to be hanged for blasphemy in Britain was Thomas Aikenhead, a 20-year-old Scotsman, executed in Edinburgh in 1697.

- In 1859, Charles Darwin finally published his theory of evolution, *On the Origin of Species*. It was quickly banned as blasphemous from the library of Trinity College, Cambridge, the university where Darwin had studied.

- The last successful prosecution for blasphemy in Britain was a private case, brought by the moral crusader Mary Whitehouse against Gay News in 1977.

The above information is reprinted with kind permission from spiked.
© spiked Ltd 2000-2023

www.spiked-online.com

'It's a culture war that's totally out of control': the authors whose books are being banned in US schools

From Art Spiegelman to Margaret Atwood, books are disappearing from the shelves of American schools. What's behind the rise in censorship?

By Claire Armitstead

When the owners of a Tennessee comics shop learned that a local school board had voted to remove Art Spiegelman's Holocaust classic *Maus* from its curriculum, they sprang into action with an appeal calling for donations to fund free copies for schoolchildren. Within hours, money started pouring in from all over the world. 'We had donations from Israel, the UK and Canada as well as from the US,' says Richard Davis, co-owner of Nirvana Comics.

Ten days later, they closed the appeal, after raising $110,000 (£84,000) from 3,500 donors. 'We bought up all the copies the publisher had in its warehouse and we're now in the process of shipping 3,000 copies of *Maus* to students all over the country, along with a study guide written by a local schoolteacher,' says Davis, who has relied on volunteers to help with the distribution.

For Spiegelman, it has meant an exponential sales boost for a 30-year-old book – the only graphic novel to win a Pulitzer prize, in 1992 – and a flurry of speaking engagements across the country. 'It just shows,' he says, 'you can't ban books unless you're willing to burn them and you can't burn them all unless you're willing to burn the writers and the readers too.'

That's just as well, adds the 74-year-old cartoonist, 'because this is the most Orwellian version of society I've ever lived in. It's not as simple as left v right. It's a culture war that's totally out of control. As a first-amendment fundamentalist, I believe in the right of anyone to read anything, provided they are properly supported. If a kid wants to read *Mein Kampf*, it's better to do it in a library or school environment than to discover it on Daddy's shelves and be traumatised.'

Unfortunately, there is an unprecedented rise in attempts to remove books from the US's libraries and schools. The American Library Association (ALA) told the *Guardian* that in the period from 1 September to 30 November, more than 330 unique cases were reported – more than double the number for the whole of 2020, and nearing the total for the previous (pre-pandemic) year.

'It's definitely getting worse,' says Suzanne Nossel, the CEO of the free-speech organisation PEN America, which has led the resistance against book banning for more than a decade. 'We used to hear about a book challenge or ban a few times a year. Now it's every week or every day. We also see proposed legislative bans, as opposed to just school districts taking action. It is part of a concerted effort to try to hold back the consequences of demographic and social change by controlling the narratives available to young people.'

Predominantly, the ALA reported, the challenges were targeted at 'the voices of the marginalised ... books and resources that mirror the lives of those who are gay, queer or transgender, or that tell the stories of persons who are Black, Indigenous or persons of colour'. Or, as Spiegelman says, of his own experience: 'If I was a transgender Black great-grandchild of slaves, I'd be more likely to be banned. This feels like a drive-by shooting.'

Maus was removed on the basis of eight swearwords – mainly 'God damn' – and nudity: a bare-breasted, suicidal mouse representing Spiegelman's mother, who killed herself when he was 20 years old. The ironic thing about it, says the cartoonist, is that he never intended the book for children, but wrote it to work out his own feelings about the parental legacy of the Holocaust. 'I was a bit offended at first when I learned that it was being used in schools, but, after speaking to young people who had read the books [it was originally published in two volumes], I just had to drop my prejudice and accept they were fine with it.'

Many of the challenges centre on a moral hysteria about the protection of children. 'They're playing woke snowflakery back: "This might upset people",' says Margaret Atwood in an email to me. A graphic novel version of Atwood's *The Handmaid's Tale* was one of the books removed from classroom libraries in a Texas school district in December, along with two other dystopian graphic novel classics: an adaptation of Shirley Jackson's *The Lottery,* and Alan Moore's *V for Vendetta*.

Texas sensitivities about *The Handmaid's Tale* are not new for Atwood, who directs me to an open letter she wrote in 2006 to a school authority after learning that it had decided to remove the novel because of sexual explicitness and offence to Christians (a decision that was overturned after impassioned representations from students). 'First,' she wrote, 'the remark: "Offensive to Christians" amazes me. Nowhere in the book is the regime identified as Christian. As for sexual explicitness, *The Handmaid's Tale* is a lot less interested in sex than is much of the *Bible*.'

Though the current censorship drive in the US is predominantly in Republican states, it has become a tit-for-tat controversy, with conservative commentators quick to point out that the left has its own form in censoring classics such as *To Kill a Mockingbird* or *Huckleberry Finn* for their perceived racist content. 'The only ones banning books are critical race theorists,' wrote the *Jewish News Syndicate* columnist Daniel Greenfield. 'Erstwhile liberals, who had once vocally championed *Huck* and *Mockingbird* and shouted down any effort to keep them out of the classroom,

now just as vocally want them out and replaced with … Ta-Nehisi Coates and Ibram X Kendi.'

Ta-Nehisi Coates's memoir *Between the World and Me*, written as a letter to his teenage son, was among more than 800 books about social justice identified for removal from Texas schools by a state legislator last year, on the basis that they were 'liable to make students feel discomfort, guilt, anguish or any other form of psychological distress because of their race or sex'. Kendi's profile, as director of the Center for Antiracist Research at Boston University and the author of three influential books on the history of racism in the US (as well as a children's book), has made him a lightning rod in the row over critical race theory, which – according to the Brookings Institute thinktank – has become 'a new bogeyman for people unwilling to acknowledge our country's racist history and how it impacts the present'.

The relationship between book challenges and attempts to control public debate is particularly obvious in this arena, with Brookings reporting in November that nine states (Idaho, Oklahoma, Tennessee, Texas, Iowa, New Hampshire, South Carolina, Arizona, and North Dakota) had already passed legislation against the teaching of critical race theory, with a further 20 either in the process of doing so, or planning to.

'We do see increased resort to censoriousness on both the left and the right,' says Nossel. 'On the left, it targets books that some people regard as racially offensive, sometimes because they originate from a different time period, when slurs were used more widely than is acceptable now. But it is the right that has invoked the machinery of government – including legislative proposals in dozens of states – to enforce these bans and prohibitions. In the hierarchy of infringements of free speech that must be recognised as more severe and alarming.'

She adds: 'There must be room for communities to debate what books and curriculum should be made available to students at various levels of education, and parents deserve a say. But ideologically driven crusades to ban particular narratives and viewpoints infringe upon open discourse in the classroom.'

It is not only in Tennessee that an alarmed progressive public has responded by pouring money into the pushback. In February, Markus Dohle, the CEO of the publisher Penguin Random House, said he would personally donate at least $500,000 to PEN America to kickstart a new fund to fight book banning, while PRH itself pledged a further $100,000.

Such high stakes might seem unthinkable in the UK, where censorship technically ended with the abolition of the Lord Chamberlain's role as theatre censor in 1968. 'Banning for swearwords – as in the *Maus* case – is a peculiarly US thing, as is banning books for sex, like Judy Blume's *Forever* was from some US state libraries for a long time,' says Julia Eccleshare, the director of the Hay children's festival. 'There are two reasons for that. One, the US still has a very active children's library service, so a collective of easy-to-rouse gatekeepers. Two, the religious right remains very powerful, so fundamentalist *Bible* teaching is still brought into arguments.'

More recently, says Eccleshare, the US has been very much on the 'front foot in attacking anything that can be interpreted as cultural appropriation or cultural insensitivity. Most tragically, I think, Laura Ingalls Wilder's *Little House on the Prairie* series has fallen from being a national treasure to being shunned, because of the Native Americans being described as frightening.'

In the UK, she adds, 'there are rarely these public "bans", with the exception perhaps of the *Little Black Sambo* books, which were quite publicly removed from library shelves'.

Back in 2003, the author Anne Fine tried to use her influence as children's laureate to get Melvin Burgess's young-adult novel *Doing It* junked by its publisher, on the grounds of obscenity, but only succeeded in increasing its sales.

'Plenty of books go out of print because they are no longer politically acceptable, and we do quietly remove books,' says Eccleshare. 'It's usually to do with racism, because we have changed such a lot in how we think. Enid Blyton's original *Noddy* stories vanished years ago, on account of their obvious racism. Similarly, *Tintin in the Congo* is only available now from very shady booksellers on the web.'

The reasons for book banning have fluctuated over history, but fall roughly into three categories: religion, obscenity and political control. In 213BC, the Chinese emperor Qin Shi Huang buried 460 scholars alive and burned all the books in his kingdom so he could control how history would remember his reign (his distant successor Xi Jinping blocked the name Winnie-the-Pooh from social media sites after being compared to the tubby bear). The first list of books forbidden in Christianity was issued by the pope in the fifth century. And, in 1749, more than a century before the Obscene Publications Act was introduced in the UK, the writer John Cleland was charged with obscenity for *Fanny Hill: Memoirs of a Woman of Pleasure*, a pornographic moneyspinner he wrote while languishing in a debtor's prison.

DH Lawrence's *Lady Chatterley's Lover* had been available in France and Italy for more than 30 years before it was published in the UK in 1960, whereupon its publisher, Penguin, was prosecuted. After a six-day trial at the Old Bailey, during which the book's defenders included the novelist EM Forster and the critic Raymond Williams, the jury found *Lady Chatterley's Lover* to be not obscene. On the first day it was available, a month later, all 200,000 copies sold.

The *Lady Chatterley* case also demonstrates the international reach of censorship, with separate obscenity trials in Japan, Australia, Canada, India and the US (where it was exonerated along with *Fanny Hill* and Henry Miller's *Tropic of Cancer*). But, it is in the political arena that book banning is now most toxic globally, with writers themselves under threat, in some parts of their world, along with their books.

The UK is the refuge for two novelists banned from their homelands, who still write in their languages of origin. Hamid Ismailov won the EBRD literature prize in 2019 with *The Devil's Dance*, the first Uzbek novel to be translated into English. Ismailov fled Uzbekistan in 1992 because of what the authoritarian state described as his 'unacceptable democratic tendencies' and worked for the BBC for 25 years. *The Devil's Dance* was smuggled into the country. 'I'm the most widely published Uzbek, yet nobody can mention any of my books. Nobody can mention my name in any article, review [or] historic piece. It's a total ban of my name, of activity, of books, of existence. It's as if I'm nonexistent,' he has said.

His most recent novel, *Manaschi*, offers a unique perspective on the colonisation by stealth of former parts of the Soviet empire by China – and also of the complex geopolitical legacy that has led to conflicts such as that playing out in Ukraine. 'It's a part of post-Soviet history that is unravelling. In the initial aftermath of the USSR breakup, many were surprised by how peacefully it happened – let's say in comparison with the breakup of Yugoslavia,' he says. 'But the Soviet Union left lots of knots, like the border issues, diasporas, ethnic minorities, mixed populations that are quite explosive in the framework of ethnic states, which inherited that legacy.'

The writer Ma Jian has been in exile from mainland China since 1987, when he published a collection of short stories based on his travels in Tibet, which was immediately banned. Until 2008, he says, his novels were published in Hong Kong, but since then they have only been available in Taiwan. By the time he finished his most recent novel, 2018's *China Dream*, even the underground bookshops in Hong Kong that had quietly imported his work had been shut down. 'Every Hong Kong publisher I approached turned *China Dream* down. They said if they did publish it, they'd lose their jobs, and, anyway, there were no bookshops left in Hong Kong that would dare sell it.'

Such international examples offer an ominous clue as to where the censorship surge in the US could lead, says Nossel. 'In the 20th century, the South African apartheid state banned 12,000 books, at one point commandeering a steel factory furnace in order to burn reviled texts. And, in the 1930s, the Nazi party railed against "un-German books", staging book burnings of Jewish, Marxist, pacifist and sexually explicit literature.'

Legislation adopted in Hungary last year banned from schools all books referencing homosexuality, in the name of the 'protection of children'. In 2014, Russia passed a law adding Nazi propaganda to the subjects it bans and restricts – 'LGBT content, offences to traditional values, and criticisms of the state are among others,' says Nossel. 'Booksellers were so fearful of running afoul of the broad law that they removed Spiegelman's *Maus* from stores because of the swastika on the book's cover, despite its potent anti-fascist message.'

'This is a book about memory,' said Spiegelman at the time. 'We don't want cultures to erase memory, because then they just keep doing the same thing again and again.'

The symmetry between Russia and the US is striking. As Oscar Wilde once wrote: 'The books that the world calls immoral are books that show the world its own shame.'

22 March 2022

Design

Design a poster promoting freedom of expression. Create a catchy slogan to go with it. Think about where would be the best places to display your poster and why.

The above information is reprinted with kind permission from *The Guardian*.
© 2023 Guardian News and Media Limited

www.theguardian.com

Whistleblowing and freedom of expression: personal rights and public wrongs

Protect Legal Adviser Isaac Heather highlights the significant gaps in UK law when it comes to protecting free expression.

As we continue to see tragedy unfolding in Ukraine, much of our day-to-day activity rightly feels utterly diminished in both its relevance and its significance.

One facet, one truth, one value that has had its fundamental significance once again highlighted though is the importance of the right to freedom of expression.

Blink and you'll miss another series of reports on new forms of censorship, fresh penalties for challenging the narrative, and increased attempts to limit the free exchange of information, views, and ideas. Among many, many other things, Russia's invasion of Ukraine can give us pause to reflect on the foundational role free speech has in contributing to a healthy society and a healthy democracy.

Just as there are profound links between free expression and democracy, between free expression and the rule of law, at Protect we believe that so too is there a fundamental link between freedom of expression and whistleblowing. And that just as freedom of expression is important for us all in many contexts, so is whistleblowing critical at every level.

By its very nature, whistleblowing involves speaking up about wrongdoing in such a way that people or organisations may wish to interfere with the act of expression. Nobody likes to receive bad news. It is never easy to admit mistakes and so there can be a temptation to shoot the messenger rather than tackle the message. In many instances this will be particularly significant as there may be a power imbalance between a whistleblower and those wishing to stop them speaking up, be that a manager, senior individual, or the organisation responsible for employing the whistleblower itself.

The true value of all free expression rights is that they help to address power imbalances to try to stop those speaking up simply being silenced by a more powerful party, be that a senior manager, a large company, or a corrupt government. This is true of whistleblowing protections too. It is therefore no surprise that whistleblowing can be, and is, understood as an exercise of the right to freedom of expression.

This is not just a theoretical point. In the UK, people have a human right to freedom of expression (enshrined in Article 10 of the Human Rights Act) and an employment right not to be mistreated for whistleblowing (found in PIDA – the Public Interest Disclosure Act). Often, a worker seeking to rely on their whistleblowing rights may only be interested in the scope of PIDA. Some individuals though are not straightforwardly protected by PIDA, including 'office holders' like judges. However, in 2019 the UK Supreme Court extended PIDA protection to judges holding that they should be granted whistleblowing protection in order to give effect to their right not to be discriminated against in the enjoyment of their right to freedom of expression under Article 10 and Article 14 of the European Convention of Human Rights.

This is a welcome acknowledgement from the country's highest judicial authority that whistleblowing engages the right to freedom of expression and that there may be instances where an individual whistleblower's legal position is enhanced by human rights considerations. Whether this could have broader implications for others who currently lack protection remains to be seen.

Whistleblowing is about more than the individual who speaks up though. Whistleblowing is about potential wrongdoing being highlighted, harm being prevented or exposed, and the public interest being served. We see this regularly in the advice line, whether it's raising concerns about health and safety in a care setting or monetary malpractice in a financial services firm. The links between freedom of expression, whistleblowing, and the public interest are clear and significant. And that's something that's true at every level, whether it's exposing high level corruption or smaller-scale harm in an everyday workplace.

Where does this leave us? Perhaps it leaves us acknowledging that there is much to do to improve the protections for whistleblowers in the UK while also appreciating the rights, protections and values that do exist. It may leave us realising more than ever how crucial strengthening these rights is for empowering otherwise vulnerable individuals to speak up in the face of authority.

Working out the contours of these rights can be difficult. But perhaps it is easier when we see whistleblowing and freedom of expression rights for what they are: fundamental personal rights, the exercise of which has the potential to prevent very public wrongs.

23rd March 2022

The above information is reprinted with kind permission from Protect.
© 2023 Protect

www.protect-advice.org.uk

Useful Websites

www.bigbrotherwatch.org.uk

www.bylinetimes.com

www.equalityhumanrights.com

www.independent.co.uk

www.inews.co.uk

www.journalism.co.uk

www.kcl.ac.uk

www.liberties.eu

www.news-decoder.com

www.ohchr.org

www.politico.eu

www.protect-advice.org.uk

www.spiked-online.co.uk

www.spectator.co.uk

www.telecoms.com

www.telegraph.co.uk

www.theconversation.com

www.thecritic.co.uk

www.theguardian.com

www.vpnoverview.com

www.yougov.co.uk

Further reading

References

From page 23:

BBC News. (n.d.). Reality Check News - BBC News. [online] Available at: https://www.bbc.co.uk/news/reality_check [Accessed 12 Apr. 2021].

Carmichael, F. and Goodman, J. (2020). Vaccine rumours debunked: Microchips, "altered DNA" and more. BBC News. [online] 15 Nov. Available at: https://www.bbc.co.uk/news/54893437 [Accessed 12 Apr. 2021].

Fox, C.S. and Saunders, J. (2020). Media Ethics, Free Speech, And The Requirements Of Democracy. Chapter: Fake News and the Limits of Freedom of Speech. S.L.: Routledge.

Givens, C. (2020). Perspective | The key to combating conspiracy theories about coronavirus vaccines. Washington Post. [online] Available at:

https://www.washingtonpost.com/outlook/2021/02/01/key-combatting-conspiracy theories-lies-about-coronavirus-vaccines/ [Accessed 12 Apr. 2021].

Goodman, J. and Carmichael, F. (2020). Coronavirus: False and misleading claims about vaccines debunked. BBC News. [online] 25 Jul. Available at:

https://www.bbc.co.uk/news/53525002 [Accessed 12 Apr. 2021].

McIntyre, L.C. (2018). Post-Truth. Mit Press.

Me Too (2018). Me Too Movement. [online] Me Too Movement. Available at: https://metoomvmt.org/ [Accessed 12 Apr. 2021].

Nix, E. (2019). Tuskegee Experiment: The Infamous Syphilis Study. [online] HISTORY. Available at: https://www.history.com/news/the-infamous-40-year-tuskegee-study [Accessed 12 Apr. 2021].

Pomerantsev, P. (2019). To Unreality–and Beyond. Journal of Design and Science, [online] (6). Available at: https://jods.mitpress.mit.edu/pub/ic90uta1/release/4

Smith, A. (2020). Facebook to ban anti-vaxx conspiracy theories. [online] The Independent. Available at: https://www.independent.co.uk/life-style/gadgets-and tech/covid-vaccine-facebook-conspiracy-ban-b1765703.html [Accessed 12 Apr. 2021].

Spangler, T. (2020). YouTube Bans COVID-19 Vaccine Conspiracy Theories and Misinformation. [online] Variety. Available at:

https://variety.com/2020/digital/news/youtube-bans-covid-vaccine-conspiracy theories-misinformation-1234804376/ [Accessed 12 Apr. 2021].

www.youtube.com. (2020). URGENT INFORMATION ON COVID VACC1NES BY DR. CARRIE MADEJ. [online] Available at:

https://www.youtube.com/watch?v=dBvY9x2Nma0&t=391s [Accessed 12 Apr. 2021].

Glossary

Cancel culture
Cancel culture is a form of boycott. An individual or organisation considered to have said something objectionable or offensive is subject to mass-shaming and shunning. This is usually performed on social media.

Censorship
When there are restrictions on what people can see or hear and on the information they are allowed to access, this is called censorship. By censoring something, an individual, publication or Government is preventing the whole truth from coming out or stopping something from being heard or seen at all. Items may also be censored or restricted to protect vulnerable people such as children, and to prevent public offence.

Classifications
Also called age ratings. Films in cinemas and on DVD as well as computer games must carry a classification indicating a minimum age at which the material should be watched or played. It is a criminal offence for a retailer to supply an age-restricted DVD or game to someone below the required age.

Culture wars
A cultural conflict between social groups who hold different beliefs, values, philosophies, etc. Usually, these disagreements are between those with 'conservative' views and those with 'progressive' views.

Fake news
Fake news is false information, often spread by the internet, usually on social media, but sometimes by other media, that appears to be true but is false. Sometimes it is done for financial or political gain,

Fourth estate
A term used to refer to the news media and its powerful, influential role in the political process.

Free press
A free press is one of which is not censored or controlled by a government. It allows us to find out what we want to know without restrictions.

Freedom of expression
Also called freedom of speech, free speech. This is protected by Article 19 of the Universal Declaration of Human Rights, which states that: 'Everyone has the right to freedom of opinion and expression; this right includes freedom to hold opinions without interference and to seek, receive and impart information and ideas through any media and regardless of frontiers'.

Gagging order
A ruling which prevents certain information from being made public. For example, if a court case is ongoing, the press can be prevented by law from publishing some of the details if it is felt it would affect the outcome of the case – i.e. by influencing the jury and therefore preventing the defendant from having a fair trial.

Ofcom
The independent regulator for all radio, television and telecom broadcasting in the UK. Ofcom deals with all the consumer complaints regarding television or radio, issue broadcasting licences and promote competition. Ofcom is Government-approved and acts under the Communications Act 2003.

Press Complaints Commission
The PCC is a regulatory body responsible for ensuring that UK newspapers and magazines adhere to a Code of Practice. The Code aims to ensure responsible journalism by setting down rules on matters such as accuracy in reporting, privacy intrusion and media coverage of vulnerable groups. If a member of the public is affected by unfair media coverage, they can complain to the PCC citing which part of the Code of Practice they feel has been breached. The Code was laid down by newspaper editors themselves, and the PCC consists of representatives of the major publishers: thus the newspaper industry is self-regulating.

The Freedom of Information Act
The Freedom of Information Act states that there should be free access to information about the Government, individuals and businesses.

The watershed
The watershed is the name for the 9pm cut-off point in television scheduling, after which television channels can show programmes containing material which may not have been suitable for a younger audience, such a scenes of a sexual nature or swearing.

Whistleblowing
You're a whistleblower if you're a worker and you report certain types of wrongdoing you have seen at your workplace. The wrongdoing you disclose must be in the public interest. Whistleblowers are protected by law and should not be treated unfairly or lose their job.

Index

A

arts, and free speech 34–35, 38

B

Bill of Rights 6–7
blasphemy 8, 36–37
book-banning 38–40
book-burning 9, 36
British Empire, views on 11, 12

C

cancel culture 7–10, 12–13, 43
censorship
    definition 43
    financial 15–17
    in football 24–27
    internet 1–3
    and social media 2, 4–5, 23
    see also free speech; press freedom
Cleanfeed 2
conspiracy theories 22–23
Counter Terrorism Internet Referral Unit (CTIRU) 2
culture wars 43

D

Digital Economy Act 2017 1
direct action protests 7
discrimination 11
disinformation 32

E

Equality Act 2010 15–16

F

fake news 22–23, 43
financial censorship 15–17
football, and censorship 24–27
freedom of expression 32–41, 43
Freedom of Information Act 2000 43
free press 18–30, 43
free speech 5–9, 12–15, 23, 34
    see also freedom of expression
Free Speech Union 15–17

G

gagging order 43
Galileo 36

H

hate speech 2, 12, 29
Human Rights Act
    Article 10 33, 41
    Article 19 18, 29, 43
hunt saboteurs 7

I

immigration 11
internet
    access 1, 4
    censorship 1–3
Investigatory Powers Act 2016 1, 2

L

LGBT issues 11

M

Milton, John 8–9

N

Nayler, James 8
Nobel Peace Prize 28

O

Ofcom 43
Online Safety Bill 4–5, 7
opinion 33
    see also freedom of expression

P

parental control filters 1
PayPal 15–17
piracy 2
pornography, online 1
Press Complaints Commission (PCC) 43
press freedom 18–30
propaganda 1–2
protests 7
Public Order Bill 7
public order offences 7

Q

Qatar World Cup, censorship 24–27

R

racism 5
religion 8–9, 11, 36–37
Reporters Without Borders (RSF) 29, 31
Rights Removal Bill 7
Rushdie, Salman 35–36

S

social media
    censorship 2, 4–5, 23
    and fake news 22–23
    see also press freedom
Spinoza, Baruch 8

T

Terrorism Act 2006 1–2
terrorist content 1–2
torrenting 1–2
transgender issues 11, 12

U

university
    and cancel culture 13
    and free speech 13–14

V

Virtual Private Networks (VPNs) 2–3

W

watershed 43
whistleblowing 41, 43
World Press Freedom Day 30